How to Develop The Faith That Heals

Fenwicke Lindsay Holmes

Printed in the United States of America

ISBN: 1481283774
ISBN-13: 978-1481283779

CONTENTS

INTRODUCTION

A NEW world dawns for us every morning. Everything in it is fresh and unknown. To the hopeful and daring soul, each day is a thrilling adventure. What it will bring, he does not know. That it will be good, he can but believe. This belief is his faith. We all live by faith for we are always on the borderland of the future. Each act is an act of faith — a feeling beforehand that the thing we are doing will bring results of some sort and usually of the kind that we expect. And the deeper this feeling is , the more certain are the results. This is especially true in the work of healing and acquiring success through the avenue of faith. No one today doubts that there is a faith that heals. What we all want is more of

THE HEALING CONSCIOUSNESS

We desire not merely to know that such a faith is possible, but to have the faith. It will, I feel sure, be an inspiration to my readers to know that it is possible to use the law of mind not only to secure what we desire, but also to develop the faith by which we speak the word that heals. How many of us have shared the experience of the father who said to the Master Healer, "If thou canst do anything, have compassion on us and help us." "If thou canst!" echoes the astonished Healer. "Why, all things are possible to him that believeth!"

"Yes," thinks the despairing father, "to him that believes, but how shall I get this faith?" Then he cries out, "Lord, I believe; help thou mine unbelief. " What he really meant was what you and I mean, "I know it is possible. Help me to know it will be done."

It is to show how faith can be acquired by the same law as health itself that this book has been written. In it, I have told as simply as possible the law of the healing consciousness, showing it to be in perfect harmony with true knowledge and the science of nature and of mind; showing how results are secured by simply knowing the truth or the law, and how we may use the same law to demonstrate faith itself. It comes out of my own heart and experience, and if it enters helpfully into yours, I shall be glad. What we are all after is not intellectual persuasion but spiritual realization. "If any man lack wisdom, let him ask of God who giveth to all men freely and upbraideth not."

Fenwicke Lindsay Holmes,

Los Angeles, Cal., October 15, 1919

(It should be noted that, in this book, "consciousness" is used in two ways. First it means the knower or personal self; and second, it means that self in the act of knowing or being aware of anything. Healing consciousness, for example, would be knowing health. Says Calkins in "Persistent Problems of Philosophy," page 407, "Consciousness, the personal idealist insists, is a conscious self or person, that is, a unique 'real' which is conscious and which may be regarded as including ideas, but which is more permanent than ideas are, and independent of them. . . . With Descartes, Berkeley, Leibniz, and Kant, Fichte, and Hegel, Lotze and Renouvier, Bergson and Eucken, Howison, Ward, and Royce, and a great company of philosophers, the writer finds that consciousness is not mere ideas or series of ideas, but that it is the unique subject of ideas.")

PART 1: THE LAW AND HOW TO USE IT

CHAPTER 1: THE NEW CONSCIOUSNESS

IT is easier to meet the situations of life, if we understand. It is ignorance that keeps us in fear. It is the unknown that haunts us and lays its ghostly fingers upon us. For life to be at all livable, we must know something about it, since thought affects not only our immediate mental states but also the people and things by which we are surrounded. And unless our thoughts are right, our world cannot be right. There are, then, certain questions upon which we must have decisive convictions if we are to be happy in the fullest way. There is little pleasure in an uphill trail if we do not know from whence we came, whither we are going, nor why we are on our way.

I feel sure that, for all of us who are thoughtful, all these questions are related to what we believe or do not believe about the nature of the self and God. Most of us feel that to be able to relate ourselves with an Unseen but not Unknown Presence will go far to put us on the pathway of understanding and so of peace and attainment.

To understand God and his way of working, is to understand our own self, since we are firmly enveloped in the Cosmic Consciousness from which our own consciousness springs, as we shall see. Or we may turn this about and say, that, to know the self in its truest and widest nature will bring us into a clearer knowledge of God. Then to know God and the self will help us to answer these big questions which confront the thoughtful heart: Is life worth while? Is there a purpose which this life fulfils or is intended to fulfil? What power have I to control the conditions of my body and environment? Is there magic in the realm of thought? Whither do I go? Can I extract joy out of existence? Can I have health when I seek it: prosperity aside from mere chance: and happiness independent of rare good luck? In short, is there a law of life?

THE SELF AND CONSCIOUSNESS

1

When we speak of consciousness, we mean the power to think; we mean the ability to be aware of the self and of that which occurs in relation to the self. The word "conscious" comes from the Latin words, cum or with, and scio, to know or have knowledge. When we say one is conscious of a thing we mean that he is "with knowledge of that thing, " at least to the extent of his being aware that it is. And the "consciousness" of a person is the "knower," or that which, within him, knows. The knower is the self, the "I am." There is neither any proof that there is an "I am," nor any knowledge of what it is in its ultimate nature. Yet, if I know anything at all, I know that I am; and I must either say that I do not know anything at all, or else say that what I know can only be known because I, the knower, exist before that which I know. How could anything be known unless there were an "I," that is, a self to know it?

This may seem very involved; but it is also very important because it shows us that "consciousness" or the knowing self exists before the body. Before the physical Jesus was the spiritual self, forever existent; the Master himself said, "Before Abraham was, I am." It is true that scientists once said that consciousness is a product of the brain, and that physical reactions in the brain cause us to think. They have claimed this because some kind of action does occur in the brain when we think. For example, if I hurt my feet, the nerve telegraph wires carry a vibration to the brain; and the message is recorded in a certain area by a little cell-shock or explosion. Then I say, "It hurts" and withdraw my feet. Now, my thought about the hurt and the cell action in the brain occurred at the same time; but that does not prove that my brain produced the thought. "I," the self, the consciousness, simply noted it; that is all. But again scientists said, "We know that it is the brain that produces consciousness because, when anything happens to any portion of the brain, we cannot think the things which that particular part of the brain is accustomed to think." In other words, we lose our consciousness to that extent. For example, they said, "Suppose I injure the brain center in which my hearing is recorded. My ear may remain as perfect; but I have lost that part of 'me' or the consciousness which hears because that part, of the brain is injured. So that, if I continue to lose parts of the brain, the 'I' would disappear little by little until it would be lost altogether."

On the contrary, other scientists call attention to the fact that the brain is merely the instrument of the consciousness and that whatever happens to it merely affects the power of the instrument but not of the consciousness. For example, if my eye is injured, the self can no longer use it as an instrument; but the self is not injured. If I break the lens of my binoculars, I cannot see through them ; but I am still a "seer." And that the self still exists after an injury to the brain, with its hearing and seeing consciousness intact, is shown by the fact that often the brain and cell life learn to use other agencies than the eye and ear to do the work that "I," the conscious self, wants done. Take, for illustration, the finer sense of touch which the blind man develops. It enables him to read, to get messages through his fingers from your lips, and to find his way about. He did not lose his seeing consciousness. He merely lost one of its instruments; his consciousness immediately set to work to find another.

The fact is that we are safe in saying that, if we cannot prove just what the consciousness is in its essence, we can say that it is, and how it works. And the greatest of the scientists today are assisting us in showing a pre-existent self or consciousness.

We find, too, that the search for the self or consciousness is not to be ended by concluding that it has taken up a temporary habitation in the body any more than we can say that a man is inseparable from his house merely because he is at home. To find what the nature of the self is, we must look beyond the body; and our study will necessarily lead us into an investigation of the universe in which consciousness finds one of its fields of expression. What is the nature of the world in which we live? Are we related to it organically only or in some higher way? Is there a consciousness back of it? If so, what is its nature? In short, what is the Cosmic Consciousness?

CHAPTER 2: COSMIC CONSCIOUSNESS

PHYSICAL science is making enormous advances today; no student of life can afford to be ignorant of the marvelous discoveries of the present hour. All the old landmarks are being swept away; a new spirit and a new order is at hand. Take, for example, the once fundamental law of physics, — the indestructibility of matter. Today we know that matter can be resolved into energy so completely that the energy will not again come back into form.

Photographs can be taken of the atoms of which material substance is composed. Yet these atoms are merely vibration. The experiments of Le Bon, the French scientist, go further than this. They show that another so-called fundamental law of physics must go by the board, — the conservation of energy. This law claimed that even when substances are entirely changed in their nature by corrosion, decay, or fire, the energy in them still exists, simply having been converted from one form into another. But Le Bon states that energy can be entirely devitalized and returned into nothingness. This means that it is no longer in shape to be perceived by the physical senses. But this "nothingness" may go under any name we wish to call it, — "The Unknown," the ether, the imponderable. Physical science thus shows us that the universe appears and disappears, evolving from and dissolving into a silent sea of an immaterial somewhat.

What is this "immaterial somewhat"? Science says it is ether, everywhere existing, without bounds, continuous, homogeneous, never dissociated in parts in which one mass of ether would be separate from another. Out of this ether, the visible universe is evolved through some activity of energy. Whence this energy and how it acts are questions which can be answered, not by physics but by metaphysics.

THE UNIVERSE CREATED BY
AN ACT OF WILL

Metaphysics is in harmony with the postulates of science when it says that energy is produced by the action of a Will; but it goes still further and says that to will is to think, that thinking is an act of mind, and that the ether of science is, therefore, better termed "Mind." For Mind, too, is spaceless, timeless, continuous, homogeneous, never dissociated in parts. In other words, it is as eternally ONE as is the ether.

Then the act of will which produces energy is the act of Mind; or, in other words, energy is this action of thought. Mind creates energy by thinking; and energy forms the substance of the visible universe. That is why we can say that the universe is "alive" for it is made by Intelligence out of Itself. No less prominent a scientist than a former president of the American association, Edward Drinker Cope, affirms that we live in a "conscious universe" and that "energy can be conscious." And he further says that "we are not necessarily bound to the hypothesis that protoplasm is the only substance capable of supporting consciousness." In other words, he perceives that consciousness and intelligence are not bound up in a physical universe or a physical body. Consciousness exists apart from all that we can examine with the five senses. It exists before creation and after.

It is not going too far to say, then, that creation is the body of God. Yet, as it would be absurd to say that the powers of man's mind are confined to his body, so is it absurd to say that all there is of God is bound up in the physical and visible universe. As all the forces of my mind can be converged to one intense point of interest, so can all the powers of the Divine Mind be brought to apply to any task which It may seek to perform. Perceiving that there is a universal intelligence apart from all limitations of time and space, we must conclude that Divine Mind can and does act, with limitless or infinite power, on its own thought. For since physical energy is but the emergence into expression of the Divine thought, for God to think is to act. When Mind acts, it is with limitless intelligence, since it is the All-Mind: It acts with limitless freedom since, as the Universal, It can have nothing outside Itself to constrain it to act contrary to its own desire. Being the homogeneous, non-dissociable, limitless One, It can have no rivals; and there is no place in the Universe for any spirit or Being contrary to Its Nature. "If God be for us, who can be against us! "Thus, when we speak of the "Cosmic Consciousness, " we are speaking of the omnipotent, omniscient, omnipresent One, whom we call God.

THE NAMES OF GOD

Is there any advantage in using this other term for God or our

Father? Only that it may bring home to us a new meaning and confidence. Whatever our earlier experience may have found in God, whatever peace, poise, faith, hope, and companionship there has been for us in the God of our earlier faith, can only be beautified and intensified by a deeper knowledge of His nature. And we can say with a greater intimacy of knowledge, "I know him in whom I have believed." The Cosmic Consciousness is the Infinite Spirit of Intelligence that "made and rules the summer flowers and all the worlds that people starry space." A mystery of being? Yes, but no more a mystery than we find on every hand. We explain physical action and reactions as due to chemical affinity, capillary action, attraction of gravity, and so on, and think we have explained; but have we? What are these forces? What is force? Can any materialist among the scientists tell us? Only a true recognition of the mental nature of the universe can answer this question. This, at least, the mental scientist can say: If we are to judge by the way they act, force and thought are the same thing. There is no distinction between what we call force and what we call thought, for force is Mind at work; and Mind at work is thought.

It is plain then that the Cosmic Consciousness is Intelligence: for it acts by thought: it is Life, for all life is derived from it: it is Wisdom, for wisdom is harmonious action; and Spirit, as One, cannot know friction from another Will: it is therefore Harmony: It is Beauty, for beauty is merely the orderly arrangement of parts: It is Love, for love is the unity of kindred things: It is all that man calls "good." And yet we must not confound this good with any idea of contrast as over against anything that we call bad, for that introduces two forces into the universe, God and a Devil, and to admit a Devil is to admit not a unitary universe, but a dualistic; and we have just seen that the universe is one. Jesus himself called attention to this as of the first importance. The greatest and first saying of the Mosaic law, said he, is this, "Hear Israel, the Lord, thy God, the Lord is one, and beside Me there is no other."

Accordingly by Good, we mean that which is real or true and that God as the Real and the True is the author of all that makes life beautiful, happy, and satisfying. And by the same token, we must perceive that what we call "bad" is merely failure to work in harmony with the law of the Good. Evil, then, is wrong thinking, the thing of a day. Truth is harmonious action, the thing of eternity. The one passes away, the other endures.

The Cosmic Consciousness is therefore everything that is true, eternal, enduring. And thinking of God in these terms of intelligence and bigness, ready to become to us just what we ask or think, we dare to launch our desire into the infinite, knowing that our vessel will return laden with the cargo which our faith has collected.

CHAPTER 3: PERSONAL AND IMPERSONAL CONSCIOUSNESS

THE Cosmic Consciousness is the all of everything of which we know. It is all of life, love, truth, and power. It includes everything within itself. There is nothing whatever outside of it. Whatever exists, therefore, must be explained in relation to it. Whatever form appears, whatever expression of life we may find, must be within the One even though it exists or stands forth as distinct from others forms. It is easier to understand this when we realize that All is Mind and that different forms are merely different thoughts put into expression. Thus the same spirit manifests in the stone, the rose, the bird and the man. Yet man himself must be explained as other than a thought of God, for he himself is a thinker; he is not only conscious but self-conscious. He thinks of himself as apart from any other self. He has individuality, that is, he conceives that there is an "I" and another that is not I. God does not have individuality in that sense: He cannot recognize another outside of Himself, for there is no outside. Thus we cannot attribute personality to God* in the ordinary limited sense of the term, for personality must necessarily imply limitation; and He is the Limitless One.

(Note: This statement often causes offense at first because not fully understood. If it is a problem to you, turn at once to Part II, Chap. 2, and read about the impersonal law and the Personal God, or read my "Being and Becoming," pages 22-25, and "Law of Mind in Action," pages 166-171. It is the highest joy of the soul to awake to this enlarged concept of God and to find our place In the Cosmic Mind.)

Personality indicates, not only separation, but also all those other attributes which we connect with it; choices of will apart from law; passions, prejudices, conflicts of opinion, purposes at variance with others, in short, all those qualities which mythology attributed to its gods. They grew angry, they fought, they sought revenge, they played favorites, they ate and drank, and granted or withheld their favors as their fickle will desired. Such a concept of God was held by the ancient peoples of the Bible; and many people today think of Him merely as an enlarged theologian, sitting on the rim of the heavens and passing judgment upon mankind.

Such a concept of personality is impossible to those who recognize God as the Cosmic or Universal Consciousness. Being intelligence or consciousness, Spirit exists independent of time and space: it has no purposes apart from the law of its being: it acts not by choices of will but by law: it is the power that stands back of everything that appears; for we are told in Scripture "the things that are seen are not made from that which doth appear." In other words, Spiritual or the Cosmic Consciousness must be recognized as the Thinker that conceives things, the substance of which they are composed, and the power that sustains them. As the water of the sea enters here to become a harbor, there to become a canal; in one place to be the ice upon the bosom of the bay, in another to be the foam of the breaking wave, and yet never loses itself as the sea; so Spirit passes into all things and all minds without losing its universality.

To so perceive the Cosmic Consciousness is to learn the secret of all demonstration, for upon its impersonality is based our power to control the affairs of our life. We get a picture of this in the analogy of the wind. The wind blowing in fresh from the sea is absolutely impersonal and impartial to all. Here it enters a window and fans a fevered brow: there it turns the great wings of the mill and grinds the grain: for one it winnows the wheat, and for another it fills the sail and drives the vessel before it. One man calls it "good" because it lifts his burden; another curses it because it whirls the sand in his face. But, neither good nor bad, the wind blows full and free and becomes to each man what he allows it. Each sets his own sail, shuts his window or opens it, exposes his grain or withholds it.

"One ship drives east, and another west,
With the self-same wind that blows;
'Tis the set of the sails and not the gales
Which tells us the way it goes. "

In other words, it is clear that we may recognize in the Cosmic Consciousness the impartial, impersonal spirit with universal powers and limitless resources, acting as the substance and the energy which man may draw upon at his own will. We apply our own conditions to it. If it is love we desire, we can draw that forth out of the infinite of love, by choosing it. If it is wisdom, we can "ask of God who giveth to all men freely and upbraideth not." If life, we may choose in what form it shall express. Were the Cosmic Consciousness other than impersonal, this would be impossible, for we would be coming constantly into conflict with its will.

It is thus evident that man makes his own world by choosing that which he will have out of the universal. "Whence did he get this endowment of power? He got it from his ageless heritage in the heart and mind of the Infinite. Consciousness, from its very-nature, is that which is and was, and ever shall be. It is impossible to conceive of it as having beginning or ending in time. That is the very mystery of its nature, that it goes before all. What man is in himself, we cannot know. As he exists, or stands forth in the Infinite or Universal as a distinct point of consciousness; and, as the Universal is One, we can conceive of man only as at one with that One, and therefore as the Universal reproducing Itself in the Particular. Man is therefore coextensive with God in the potential nature of his being; and, however exalted and wild an idea this might seem in view of man's earthly history and experience, the logic of idealism, the testimony of the prophets, and the vision of the soul alike bear witness to it. Consciousness or the ego never was born, for it exists forever in the Eternal One. You, the eternal one of Spirit, have never been born, you never can die. "The kingdom of heaven is within you," said Jesus. "Now, Father, glorify thou me with Thine own self with the glory that I had with Thee before the world was: For thou lovest me before the foundation of the world." "Before Abraham was. I am." Whether the consciousness of the individual returns again and again to embody itself in brain and muscle, nerve and neuron, I do not know. That he shares in that Eternal Light that shines from eternity to eternity, is attested by every reason by which we are enabled to say that we exist at all or that there is a God.

CHAPTER 4: THE LAW OF CONSCIOUSNESS, STATED

IT has become evident from the previous chapters that man's control of body and conditions rests not in chance but on conscious choice. So soon as he acquires the new understanding, he perceives that he gets out of life just what he puts into it, "that as he thinks in his heart so is he," that he "shall ask what he will in my name (that of the real self) and it shall be done unto him." He then perceives that whatever has happened to him up to this time has not been due to chance nor the fickle favor of fortune, nor the good or bad will of God, nor man nor the devil. He perceives that he is dealing with the law, that "as a man soweth in word or deed so shall he also reap," that the Cosmic Consciousness acts as the law of life, that it is impartial and impersonal, and that "he sendeth his rain upon the evil and the good, upon the just and the unjust." These are notable discoveries. But by them a man is put upon his own resources. He has no devil to blame. There is no luck good or bad; there are no mistakes except his own; and the inharmony he feels is the inharmony he makes. We are living in a universe of pure intelligence, infinite in power, continuously creative, and impersonally manifesting in poverty or wealth, sickness or health, according to the dictates of our own selections. We set the mould into which Spirit shall pour Itself out into form for us. If we are rich, it is by no chance. Either consciously or unconsciously, we have kept the law; we have sowed faith in supply. Big men of finance tell us that they have never even thought of themselves as not having or making plenty of money. They have always expected financial success and have therefore gained it. They have expected it! In that, is the secret. Our demonstration is in the terms of our expectancy. He who anticipates poverty with dread, will eventually hear the great gaunt wolf howling at his door unless he changes his thought.

If, on the other hand, you have the perfect wealth consciousness, yet dread disease, then you are laying yourself open to its invasion. A man might keep every law of success; but violating the law of health, he would reap the fruits in ill-health of some sort. Multimillionaires are not immune to dispepsia — if they have the dispeptic consciousness.

We are free from the things we do not want, only by forgetting them and turning our thought to the things we do want. The law of consciousness reveals the fact, therefore, that we bring into our lives just what comes, by the attitude we assume toward life. Blessed is that man who expects something, for verily he shall have his reward. And he who expects nothing will get that, too.

As eagerly as water flows to fill a vacuum, so Spirit flows to every point where receptivity is provided, becoming what we think. The same substance becomes the rose and the thorn, the buttercup and the burr, the sunshine and the cloud, the rain and the rainbow; it flows through the blood as the corpuscle or the germ, and deposits as the cancer or the cure. Neutral, impartial, impersonal, it assumes the form and the quality which our own thought provides. Out of the intangible, ever-present, infinite, all-powerful substance of Spirit by which you are surrounded and in which you are immersed, you draw your bane or blessing, pain or pleasure. As the mirror takes the image you reflect into it without a murmur and without a change, so this all-encircling consciousness images your thought and puts it forth into expression. But, unlike the mirror, it is infinitely creative. It does not pass away until all is fulfilled; and unless you change the image by changing the thought, it will go on creating for you indefinitely. This is the reason why "the thing I greatly feared has come upon me." Fear has gripped the thought and the imagination. The more intense it is, the clearer is the image of the disaster which is dreaded; and, in some form or other, we draw out of the Universal the very thing that we do not want. Happy is he who knows this and carefully scrutinizes every thought and motive that he may put forth in idea only that which is beautiful and good, and bring into his life the full fruit of his bouyant faith.

Boldly must he, who makes the discovery of his own life and powers, face the issue. He may not like the situation; he may resent the responsibility. He may wish to bark back to a devil or a God to blame for his misfortunes: he may wish that he could escape the burden. He cannot. He may say with Job. "Let the day perish wherein I was born.

But he is here; and he must face the fact. One cannot avoid danger by turning his back, nor escape the light by shutting his eyes. We cannot fit Truth to us; we must fit ourselves to the truth. We cannot break the law; but we can be broken by trying to break it. He who opposes the law is ground to dust and ashes, not by its volition but his own, as a knife may be ground away against the stone. Instead of crying out against the law, we must seek to understand it. We must "know the truth; and the truth will set us free. We are bound in the chains of our own ignorance; and our escape is not by struggle but by knowledge.

CHAPTER 5: THE LAW OF CONSCIOUSNESS, OUTLINED

WHATEVER comes into our lives comes in obedience to the law of consciousness, — that what we think and feel ultimately expresses in act and form. Every mental activity is followed by some form of objectivity, for this is the very essence of its nature. It is so because the only way Mind can create is by thought; and we must recall that at the beginning of every creative series there is nothing else than a Mind to create and nothing out of which to make things but Itself. This calls attention to a number of facts with which we ought to be familiar, even at the risk of repetition.

1.   The starting point in thoughts, things, feelings, expressions, is Mind. At the beginning, there is Intelligence, ever operative, everywhere present, power of all power, life of all life. Back of every thought you think is the infinite of life, love and power.

2.   The substance of all things is consciousness or intelligence in some form. If you wish to speak of this intelligence in esoteric terms, you may call it the Word and with John may say, "In the beginning was the "Word and the Word was with God and the Word was God, and the Word was made flesh and dwelt among us." This is as true of all things and people as it was of Jesus. What we call flesh or matter or "things" is simply the crystallization into form of the thought which it expresses.

3. Cosmic Consciousness makes a world out of itself by simply speaking the Word; the Word is backed up by limitless power and intelligence; and, as you cannot think a thought without thinking it into the infinite of being (since it is one and you are in it) every word that you speak is backed up by all the power of heaven. This is why those who live in the consciousness of the Presence and whose thoughts are set on the highest, get such noble results in character and attainment. This is why those who persistently hold thoughts of fear and failure, or

13

jealousy and revenge, are ultimately overwhelmed. They have set into motion forces which they do not control; and they must bear the consequences. Only our natural selection of the better and the fact that the aggregate of our thinking is in the right direction keeps us from self-destruction. Only our failure to know the best, to believe in it, and to seek it, keeps us from rising to heights supreme and wonderful.

4. Cosmic Consciousness is continuously creative. Everywhere new things are appearing and old are passing away. New birds are born to sing, new roses to bloom, new stars to shine. The whole study of science is merely to discover what the Creative Mind is making and how It is making it. And the province of philosophy and religion is to make the new alignments of life which the new discoveries make possible. Science, philosophy, and religion cannot stand still because God does not stand still. "Behold I make all things new." Human progress is like a vessel ploughing its way through an unknown sea. Some sleep; some watch ; and some desire to put about.

When morning breaks, the wise soul peers forth to what the new day shall reveal: what course he will follow? what islands shall he see? what new continents appear? what harbors may he enter? Old things are passing away under the momentum of the advance of the race. We are in the new current; and fresh winds stir the sails. A new captain is on the deck. New leaders in all things! New rulers of men, new rulers of industry! New moulders of public opinion! New methods! New education! New religion! New powers unfolding! New opportunity! New life! A new day! A new Consciousness! What ecstasy of change for the valiant and fearless soul!

He of the big vision smiles. Is he poor? The wheel will turn, for he will turn it! Is he sick? Life shall flood to overflowing banks, for he will open the gates! Is he enslaved by fears or circumstances? He will cast off the shackles! Is he unhappy? He will find the point of friction and remove it. Does the grave threaten? He will peer beyond! He faces all, dares all, achieves all, because all things are being made new; and he is in the midst of it. If he will but sieze the tiller of his own vessel, he may seek what harbors he will; and the Cosmic Power will become at once the wind for his sail and the sea upon which he may safely adventure. He can never sail beyond the Infinite Care.

CHAPTER 6: : OUTLINE OF THE LAW OF CONSCIOUSNESS SUBJECTIVE DEFINED

COSMIC Mind, being universal, is a unit, as we have seen. As a unit, it must be independent of any consciousness of individuality, for individuality is an expression of separateness; and the Cosmic Mind cannot think of itself as apart from another, as there are no parts. This Mind is therefore subjective, because objective mind is the development of consciousness to contact a world of form and to understand and adjust to it. The babe is born practically entirely subjective; it is emerging into an objective world. So it soon develops an objective consciousness through an effort to adjust to environment. Creative Mind, however, is the originator of form, is the sustaining principle within it, has no sense of separation from it, and, therefore, does not have objective faculties. Accordingly, it does not have personality in the common meaning of the term, for personality is the sum-total of individual consciousness, including subjective and objective characteristics. The impersonal, subjective character of the Cosmic Mind must be emphasized and borne constantly in mind.* Otherwise we would be thinking of It as having purpose of its own as opposed to ours. We would think of God as fickle, sometimes answering prayer, and sometimes not. And feeling that there is a big element of chance in the answer to prayer, we should cease to pray at all. *(See Note, page 16.)

We should lose our sense of contact and drift into agnosticism and discouragement of every kind. But once conceive of Cosmic Consciousness as the impersonal, creative Spirit and act in relationship to it on that basis; and we have the foundation of a science of effective prayer.

As this may seem abstract, it is suggestive to compare with Cosmic Consciousness, the consciousness of the individual as we perceive it in the phenomenon of hypnotism. Experiments along this line have revealed that, under certain circumstances, the objective faculties can be made quiescent for a time; and the mind will then act entirely subjectively, that is, the individual puts off the conscious personality or realization of himself as a self.

He then acts under the direction of the operator and assumes the personality which is suggested to him. The objective mind and will of the operator virtually becomes his for the time. If it is suggested to him by that mind that he is a lawyer, he will begin to act on that assumption and use the terms and ape the manners of a lawyer. If it is impressed upon him that he is a great orator, he will accept the impression and frequently make a pleasing speech. The thing to note is his unquestioning, impersonal acceptance of any suggestion that is offered to him.

This singleness of idea and assumption of personality is by no means confined to hypnotism. Let any one be possessed of and by a big idea, and with singleness of purpose, he will act it out to the last degree. Joan of Arc may be used as an illustration. Impressed with the idea that heavenly voices summoned her to save the French cause, she accepted the suggestion. Her subjective faculties acted upon it to the fullest extent; and she developed into the saviour of a great cause. All lofty achievement and all fanaticism alike is based on this principle, that there is a power within us, call it subjective Consciousness or what you will, that takes the big idea of our life and builds out of the hidden resources of our soul, the power to put that idea forth into objective expression. This is the basis of psychotherapeutics with the medical profession: of suggestion and of autosuggestion with the psychologist.

PSYCHOLOGY AND METAPHYSICS

It may be interesting here to note the difference between the psychological and the metaphysical theory and practice. Psychology is the science of the individual mind; and healing is accomplished through the subjective creative mind of the individual. Metaphysics is the science of the universal mind and healing is obtained through the action of the Universal or Divine Mind. Both views are correct, as the creative, impersonal mind of the individual and the universal are one in essence and nature. "It is not I that speak; but my Father dwelling in me, He doeth the works." The difference between the two concepts is in the attitude of mind and the relative effect. We must realize, that the stronger the idea and the greater the faith, the more successful and permanent will be the results. If, then, we feel that all the forces of heaven are directly at our disposal, we are assured of a wealth of success. This the metaphysician feels; and this he seeks to impart to his patient. On the other hand, in suggestion to the individual mind, the patient cannot but hold the idea that he is intimately involved in the process, that he has something to do which involves struggle. With the idea of struggle enters the element of doubt as to the issue; doubt becomes a part, at least, of the auto-suggestion; and the consequence is frequent and dismal failure.

We must not lose sight of the point intended to be noted in this fifth section: namely, that Cosmic Consciousness, while infinitely creative, does not interfere in our affairs; and, while It is ready to become to us just what we ask and think, it does not take the initiative. It is the impersonal, creative force acting on the ideas which it presents to itself in the work of creating a visible cosmos, wherein it acts as the law of tendency, or else acting upon the ideas which are presented to it by the individual who seeks its aid.

THE VALUE OF VISION

We thus see that Cosmic Consciousness acts on the strongest idea or concept that is impressed upon it; and the importance of ideation or image formation becomes very evident to us. The life is fullest that is most replete with creative images, that ventures most in faith into the Unseen but not Unknown. And the dreamer is no longer to be despised. Dream your dreams, see your visions, picture your good, knowing that you draw forth from the inexhaustable resources of heaven just what your faith demands. Vision and faith will carry you across every sea of despair, every mountain of difficulty. Ask, with faith, believing.

A man there was, with a common name
And a common view of life:
His thoughts were always of common things
And never rose to the sky on wings,
Nor ever soared where the spirit sings
Far over the common strife.
So he lived and worked in a common way
In a plain and grubworm style;
He ate and slept with never a thought
To lift him out of the common lot;
And so, at length, in a common spot,
They laid him after a while.

Another there was with a common name,
But a vision vast and high;
He dreamed of heights for his soul to climb,
And, vision with act in perfect rhyme,
He flung himself, with a faith sublime,
Far out on the trackless sky.

He blazed a trail for the souls to come

17

With a dreamer's artless art:
For ever the dreamer of noble mind,
Who lives his vision, shall living find
His vision painted for all mankind
And hung in the common heart.

CHAPTER 7: THE PRACTICAL USE OF VISION

VISUALIZING PROSPERITY

EVEN our dreams have meaning, for they are the pictures of our desires, although often hidden from our rationalizing mind and obscured by their imagery. The study of dreams and their interpretation was a work of some of the great Bible characters like Joseph and Daniel; and, through the investigations of Freud and other psychologists, we find a recurrent interest in these interpretations. What I wish particularly to call attention to is the fact that the activity of the mind in dreams is always by way of picture-formation; its ideas are in picture-form. Our dreams are cinematographs; and, it is probable, they are entirely devoid of the element of time. It is only when we awaken that we give full cohesion to them. So rapidly do they occur, that it sometimes happens we dream in a few seconds so much that it takes many minutes to recount it when we put it into words. Men, who have all but met death by drowning, tell us that they have had a full review of their whole career pass across their mind in a flash of vision.

The lives of the mystics are replete with illustrations of the picture-forming nature of mind. When they reach an advanced state of consciousness and, in deep contemplation, become conscious of the All, they sometimes fall into a swoon during which they are visited with visions and ecstasies. From these visions, they awake with renewed zeal and physical capacities.

We may note, too, that primitive language was always in pictures of some sort, as we may see from a study of the hieroglyphics of the ancient Egyptians, Chinese, Aztecs, Peruvians, and the American Indians.

All these facts show us that in some way the initial step in consciousness is by way of pictures. The imaging faculty is not the acquirement merely of education. It is native to us. It antecedes time and belongs to the subjective life. Most people use this faculty in

19

remembering things. They have what is called a "visual memory." They remember by the way it looks. In my own experience as a student, I depended on this faculty to such an extent that I frequently quoted history and science in an examination, word for word with the page of my text-book. It often recalls the words of a speaker to think of just how he looked when he said what he did. We thus find ourselves drawing forth our memory or recollection from the primitive storehouse of the infallible memory of the picture-making mind.

Someone has said "the language of spirit is form" ; and this fact is not only borne out by what we have said of actual experience, but also by all that we can conceive of the creative method. At the beginning of creation, the Cosmic Consciousness has no objective pattern for the things it will create. Nothing has appeared in form; and the only way it can be brought forth is by the Creative Imagination of Spirit. Spirit or Mind, therefore, makes a world by simply thinking of the form which it shall assume. Its language is the language of pictures. By that divine quality inherent in Its being which we may call imagination, It starts the initial impulse of a world. It visions a sun; and it blazes into glory; It dreams; and all Its dreams come true.

VISUALIZATION

If, now, we will couple with the foregoing facts the further truth that our dream passes into thought, our thought into act and objective form, and that "we are what we think," we shall have the sure foundation for a definite method in demonstration. This is the method of visualization.

Let us suppose you want a new home. The case of a friend will illustrate the principle. He desired a better home and one more worthy of his culture and increasing capacities. He believed in his power to bring to him the good he sought and set himself definitely to work. He began to picture the kind of house he wanted. He saw it large and commodious. Here were the broad steps and the wide veranda. He mentally entered through the oak-paneled door into the attractive reception-room. He saw the rich rugs on the floor, the warm fireplace at one side, and the upholstered chairs. Then he saw himself as the master of the house, dressed in perfect taste and comfort, descending the handsome stairway on the right, and coming forward to greet a welcome guest. Thus he pictured himself in detail, living in the house of his imagination and enjoying its luxury. He saw himself as a man of affluence with money in his pocket sufficient for every need, and, in short, created by vision a new life for himself. Within a year's time, his dream was realized; and he stepped into the larger sphere which his faith had perfected. Truly, "the things that are seen are not made of that which doth appear!" "Faith is the substance of things hoped for, the evidence of things not seen." Whatsoever things ye desire when ye pray, believe that ye have received them and ye shall receive them."

Out of the invisible realms of spirit, out of that which from the physical side is "nothing" but which from the spiritual side is "everything," out of that nothing into which science can entirely dissolve matter, and yet from which all matter proceeds,* man may draw his good by simply repeating the creative process ; and this is the work of vision.

You need have no fear for the issue, if you will but have faith in the power of visualization. Let your soul articulate in form. Perceive your good inwardly and claim it. If it is money you need, see yourself in possession of it. If it is a journey you wish to take, then venture out in vision. Visualize the trip; go to Paris while still in London; visit Rome while still in Paris. But do not rest there. State firmly and with conviction, "This is the picture of what is mine. Let it be brought forth in a completeness which is above my present scope of vision." Then it "shall be done unto you above all you ask or think."

*See Chapter II.

CHAPTER 8: ON VISUALIZING SUCCESS AND KEEPING THE LAW

THE foregoing chapters have outlined the method by which we may attain. We are to recognize an Infinite Creative Consciousness, willing to become to us all we may ask or think, possessed of an intelligence not only capable of understanding our desires but also of carrying them into effect with infinite wisdom. Nor is this all, for there may be factors in the case with which we are unfamiliar and with which we may be unable to acquaint ourselves. The Cosmic Mind will see to this for us. There may be means and agencies which must be employed to realize our good of which we know or can know nothing. Spirit knows these and will provide the way in which our good shall come. We should never question the issue merely because we do not know how it should be done. This is so important that I wish to illustrate it here.

A woman, who was in financial trouble, came for help. She was carrying on business in a store where the rent was too high for the volume of her trade to support it. After several months, she found herself at the point of bankruptcy. She owed a month's rent; and, by the terms of her lease, all her fixtures, machinery, and equipment could be attached not only for the rent but also to insure the lease. She asked the owner of the building to give her a few days' time in which to try to find a purchaser of the business, whose experience and increased capital would enable him to buy her out, assume the lease, and save her from bankruptcy.

I talked with her, assuring her that while we did not know who the purchaser would be, there is an Intelligence that is in touch with all minds and does know. We then visualized the right man or men appearing in her store. Immediately she began to have enquiries about the business; and two men came who were partners in another place and were looking for an opening for enlarging their trade. One of them was very much pleased with the new location; but the other held off because he thought the rent too high.

The woman then asked if I did not think that we ought to hold in consciousness that these two men would decide to buy. I told her that while this might seem a natural thing to do, it was not in accord with the high principles of this science. It was one thing to know there were purchasers who would want the property, it was another thing to make them want it. The one was faith; the other was hypnotism. We can choose what we want; we must not choose the way it is to come; and for us to try to force the issue by subtle mental influence is the invasion of the rights of others. This is a very important fact and ought to be emphasized. People sometimes come and innocently enough, since they do not know the law, ask that we should use the law to make others give them money, or yield to them in some way. When we want anything we should choose the thing we desire and then know that it will come without robbing another or by striving to influence any one by the hidden powers of mind. If necessities of the case are such that the act of another is directly involved, — as when, for example, there is inharmony in the family, — we must affirm that such an one will act on the basis of his highest nature, that his best self will govern his actions. And, as nothing comes to us that we have not invited in some way, we should realize that instead of "treating" another to make him do the right thing; we should "treat" our self to know that no injustice can be done to us.

Accordingly, we affirmed in spirit that the business was sold; no matter who should buy it. The partners called on another firm with the intention of buying the latter's business. "We would sell to you," was the reply, "if we could find another location to suit our own growing trade." "Why don't you go to see Mrs. P —? She has a good location for you." The result was that Mrs. P — sold her business to the second party and was able to pay the rent in arrears and save her own property.

We are dealing with an Intelligence that knows all, is in Itself all substance, is able to "do exceeding abundantly above all we ask or think." We should then know that "my God is able to supply all my wants," and it is not for us to dictate how our good shall come. We can safely rest our case in the Infinite Consciousness, and thus be saved from eternal worry and fear.

CHAPTER 9: VISUALIZING HEALTH

IT is a mistake to say that man reaches out into the invisible and plucks forth what is already there. The possibility is already there, the unmanifest is potentially there, the undifferentiated of life, love and wisdom is there; but it exists in the essence from which the thing itself is to be brought into form. An acorn is not an oak; a copper mine is not a kettle. A tree is not a house, and a thought is not a book. We get out of the invisible the substance of which the thing we desire is to be made; but we mould and make the thing by our own thought. Just as a river is water diffused and undifferentiated into various forms of expression, but can here be caught into a vessel and frozen into ice, there caught into a ditch and spread out in irrigation, and in another place turned into power over the water wheel; so can Spirit be fashioned into prosperity, happiness, or a physical body. But you, the individual self, choose what the form shall be; and, although the process may be unconscious at first, as in the moulding of the body as you grow from infancy, there comes a time when you more consciously choose, both in the food you eat, the clothes you wear, and the thoughts you think.

SELECTING THE RIGHT IDEA

Knowing as we do that the thoughts we think are in the ultimate the decisive factor in eating, in methods of acting, in sanitation, and hygiene; nay, more, that all these things themselves are the manifestation of thought, and, in their real nature are thought itself, we ought to carefully select the thoughts and images which will secure for us the most delightful results. We ought to form as perfect concepts as possible. This is the value of our imaging faculty.

What is your concept of a perfect body? Cultivate an imagination about it. Deny the seeming for a time, in order that you may conceive the better thing. Imagine yourself as buoyant, elastic! See yourself as walking comfortably about or working at the vocation you enjoy!

Picture yourself as functioning perfectly within the very part of your organism that now distresses you!

A friend of mine practically overcame lameness by refusing to carry a cane and indignantly objecting to her family's habit of springing forward to aid her. She taught her nerves and muscles to do their natural work by insisting on their doing it and imagining they were working as they ought.

SEE YOURSELF IDEALLY

In the same way see yourself ideally. If you are upon a bed of sickness, begin by thinking in terms of the real self. "I, the real self, am a free spirit; I am free in mind and free in body. I can do what I will, go where I will, live as I will. This body is my servant and does as I dictate. I see myself whole and free from pain. I rise from this bed. I stand upon my feet. I am free, free, FREE! I claim my freedom!"

I know of one who used this method in healing himself of valvular leakage of the heart. He was examined by a physician who told him the nature of his trouble. Undismayed, he returned to his home and began his treatment. Every day, he laid his hand over the region of his heart and declared, "I see you functioning perfectly; I see every organ in its right place. I see my heart acting as it should." Then, he withdrew his thought from his heart and turned it to a deep realization of life. In a few months, he was again examined by the physician and declared perfectly well.

Another, who had what is called a floating kidney, caused it to become fixed in perfect order by daily seeing it in its place through the image-forming power of his mind.

It is clear how such treatment would act. The subjective, creative activity of mind has the strong impression of health stamped upon it. The objective side of mind would not know always just how the organs of the body look or function; but the deeper creative mind does know, for it built them in the first place. Each organ is an intelligence functioning without our conscious thought. But, in the case of disease, we have interfered with its activity through mental pressure of some kind, through fear or wrong thinking. If now we change the current of our thought and think of our body as functioning perfectly, the body will respond.

SEE YOURSELF AS SPIRIT

A good method is to image the body as pure spirit, to see yourself as spirit living in a world of spirit, unhampered by grosser forms called matter.

Dream yourself as existing in this pure world of spirit. You are thus seeing yourself ideally. You are seeing yourself as you are in the potential power of being. Then the creative life within you takes this idea of itself and begins to construct accordingly.

So you find that "you do not have to struggle; you only have to know." Let no one fasten upon you the thought that your trouble is incurable. Who is he that shall usurp your rights of image-formation? Who shall supplant your picture-forming power? Shall you accept his dictum? The language of creative activity is visualization, the articulation of vision is thought, the expression of thought is objective realization. Creation never ceases. Therefore do not despair before the verdict of the physician. You are the metaphysician. You are the master within the temple of your body. Have faith, only believe, and "it shall be done unto you of my Father."

CHAPTER 10: VISUALIZING HEALTH IN THE CASE OF ORGANIC DISEASE

THE CURE OF "INCURABLES"

MEDICAL science has seen fit to issue the dictum that some diseases are incurable, and to fasten this dread thought upon the mind of the patient. Sometimes such disease is organic, that is, the organ is deformed in some way rather than merely functioning wrongly. In the case of nervous diseases, the patient is frequently told, "You cannot recover. No one ever recovers from such trouble. "This places before the patient the inevitable picture of deformity and despair, and adds to the malignancy of the disease. Such cases are often encountered by the metaphysician who is called in as a last hope. He must at once set to work to destroy the wrong image by substituting for it a right one. He must realize that healing originates, not in human will but Divine Mind. It emerges from Spirit. Its forces are the forces of the eternal. Health is the outpouring of "Him who is able to do exceedingly abundantly above all we ask or think." The source is Omnipotent Mind. We have, then, an unlimited source, an unplumbed reservoir from which to draw. Nor are these forces in the hands of a miser power, an unwilling giver; for "He is more willing to give than we are to receive".

Did we but realize it, the healing forces are all about us now, pressing upon us, seeking admission at the door of mind and body. They stand at the door and knock. They search us out, for Spirit is forever seeking expression as love, joy, peace, health, intelligence, and power. We depend entirely upon the absolute source of all; we draw from the Unlimited; we secure our model from the Perfect. "We know, therefore, that all disease is curable.

Let us, therefore, with perfect confidence approach the Divine Mind. Formulate the picture of health and know that the agencies which turn your vision into flesh and bone, nerve and neuron, are already in existence. They will carry your message to the afflicted organ.

27

That organ becomes the depository of your new health forces and the substance you have drawn forth from mind. Just as the Mississippi River or the Nile build up rich deltas by bringing down from the hills and plains their rich cargoes of loam, so the inner forces of the body carry, through chosen channels, the reconstructive forces of the body, which your vision and will have ordered forth. As the river currents may be directed to any chosen locality, so these rich forces can be directed to any part of the body.

VISUALIZING THE MODEL

The forces of life are sentient; they are thought-forms; they have intelligence; each is a little workman bearing on its face the stamp of an idea. In other words, we may impress on the reconstructive forces the model of the perfect organ and tell them to build on that plan. They obey mind; they rush to do the bidding of the will. If we give them a plan of health, they build health; if of disease, they build disease. If we say, "This is the perfect idea, build to it, " they so build. The reason you are sick is that you have thought wrong thoughts; change the image and the body will change with it.

The body is but a manifestation of spirit; "matter is but spirit at its lowest level." Therefore, when you have a case of supposed difficulty, you must get into a heightened consciousness of spirit. The greatest healer is simply the one who can most completely become conscious of spirit, who can know that all is mind. He uses the same power in every case, hard or easy. He never has any harder task than to control his own consciousness. He has first of all to know that his word or thought has all power. He must rise above all ideas of difficulty, and recognize that he is dealing with a power that does not know the word difficulty or failure or incurable. He then dissolves the body into its constituent element of spirit; he sees it as spirit, poises it in the spiritual realm, deals with it as the perfect spiritual idea or perfect thought of Mind. He must see man as the perfect expression of the Perfect One.

FEELING YOUR UNITY WITH SPIRIT

You are as you think; if, therefore, you conceive of yourself as at one with this Perfect One, you will draw to your own visualized picture of health the higher idea of the Creative One. Then the creative forces will have impressed upon them the best and finest idea; and you can rest your case in Omnipotent Hands. Your bodily organs will then be conceived of as God conceived of them in the beginning. Realizing the body as spirit, an organic disease or an "incurable", one will be found to be no different from a "slight affectation." All disease is but the registry of wrong ideas upon the body; and therefore the strength of the disease is in the strength of the idea. If then, you know the truth that all is spirit and insist on its expression, you need not doubt the issue.

The strength of your idea depends upon the depth of the feeling that accompanies it. How much faith have you? How persistent is your effort? The disciples could not heal the epileptic boy. They appealed to Jesus, who, coming down from the mountain where he had realized the limitless power of God, spoke the healing word. Jesus was the perfect channel of power. To the disciples who asked why they failed, he replied, "Because of your little faith. If ye have faith as a grain of mustard seed, ye shall say unto this mountain, 'Remove hence to yonder place; and it shall remove; and nothing shall be impossible to you." Mountains of difficulty in healing move at the command of a master faith. All visualizations of healing must be accompanied by deep expectancy; and it may be encouraging now to realize that just as we can demonstrate the health or prosperity we desire through faith in the law, so we can demonstrate the faith that heals. How this can be done we will show in the second part of this book. Let us seek this faith, Expect, Expect, EXPECT!

PART II: HOW TO DEVELOP FAITH THROUGH USE OF THE LAW

CHAPTER 1: THE NEW HEALING AND PROSPERITY CONSCIOUSNESS

CONSCIOUSNESS as intelligence is neither new nor old, yet in each of us there is an awakening of the self to the powers we possess which may well be called the new consciousness. One of us widely unfolds the portals of his mind to the perception of life; and we say of him, "He has a great healing consciousness." Of another we say, "He has a wonderful consciousness of prosperity." When we enter into the deeper realization of the indwelling life, we may be said to have a new consciousness. To feel this life and the power of it to the depths of our being is to have the faith that moves the world. All of us want it. "Lord, I believe; help thou mine unbelief!" is the cry of every soul at some period of unfoldment. In itself, it expresses both a belief and a desire. The belief is, "These things can be true; I believe in them intellectually. I accept the science of it. "The desire is, "Oh, that I might have a deep feeling of the truth; that I might today know it in my heart rather than in my head!"

Do we not often hear it asked, "Why is it that I have had this accident or sickness? — I who believe all these things?" The answer is that your knowledge has not yet passed into spiritual understanding. Objectively you have accepted truth but not subjectively as yet. But the subjective or deeper consciousness is the creative faculty, and whatever is there as feeling, vision, or belief, governs your life. It is because your word has not been backed with the feeling consciousness that you have failed. This is why great teachers have not always been great healers. The early or untimely death of a great teacher is not a reason for unbelief nor reproach. Such an one may have seen clearly with the intellectual or rational eye; but he failed to have experienced the truth emotionally enough: that is, did not feel it as fact for himself. There is no moral nor intellectual fault. It is the law at work, the sun shining with equal impartiality on the evil and the good. And we must

31

remember, too, that some teachers have not wished to live longer in the body.

SPIRITUAL CONSCIOUSNESS

How then may we turn our intellectual assent into spiritual consciousness? Here is the great demand of this science. Let us see if it may not be answered by direct demonstration to this end.

All that is is brought into expression by the "word." We begin with the word; that is the definite formulation of our desire; and we set this word free in the Divine Mind. We dwell mentally on the fact that this Mind takes every word we thus put forth as its starting point and operates upon it with perfect intelligence and limitless power. It does not refuse the word; it does not ask questions; it does not argue; it does not say, "This will harm you when you get it, that other would be better." It makes no choice for you. It is law; and its nature is that "whatsoever a man soweth, that shall he also reap." "The seed is the word"; and Creative Mind takes it and begins to grow the harvest, dates from dates, figs from figs, and thistles from thistles. It grows a thorny cactus with no less interest than a fragrant lily.

By the same rule, you can develop or unfold the new consciousness. Remember that you are seeking something as definite in this desire as in any other. You would not hesitate to ask Spirit's co-operation in solving a problem in philosophy or arithmetic. Why hesitate in using the law to unfold spiritual consciousness? Spiritual attainment is only another name for high, fine mental states. Spirituality is lofty thinking, true thinking. Therefore choose your word with this in mind, "I am about to demonstrate a deeper sense of my atonement with Spirit and consequent power."

UNFOLDING YOUR CONSCIOUSNESS

Your word then is, "I know that there is but one Mind; and I am in it. Spirit can and desires to act through me. The Divine Presence wishes to recognized. Love, light and wisdom can spring forth from within me as water bursts forth to spray the fountain. Thou Mind of the World, Thou doest take the things of the spirit and manifest them unto me; Thou doest take my word and bring forth my desire into expression in health and prosperity. But most of all would I have Thee manifest Thyself to me in the deepened consciousness of my atonement with Thee, to such an extent that when I speak the word, I am no longer filled with doubt, to such an extent indeed that I shall unquestioningly feel that 'heaven and earth shall pass away; but this my word, shall not pass away until all be fulfilled.'"

"Now do I have that serene consciousness that is sure of the fact that thought controls substance and passes it out into form. Now do I feel, deep within my being, that the things I desire shall come to pass. I not only know that these things can be but that they will be. I am conscious of the fact that I and the Father are one. He is creative; I am creative: He is changeless substance; I am changeless substance: He is eternal ; I am eternal : He is perfect ; I am perfect : He is complete ; I am complete. As He creates by thinking, so do I. I am conscious of myself as self-directing. I have faith; I believe in the power of my own word to bring things forth out of the invisible."

TO EMBODY IN CONSCIOUSNESS

To embody things in consciousness is to unquestioningly feel that when we speak the word, "it is done unto us even as we will." It stands forth completed in spirit; its soul goes forth to take on its body. It is done so far as we are concerned; it will appear objectively at such time and place as it is needed, now or later.

To acquire the embodying consciousness is therefore of all things desirable. To this end, we may practice concentration and wisely seek to realize the presence of Spirit in all our affairs; but I know of no way more sure of getting quick and sure results than that already outlined, by which we simply declare into Divine Mind that we have the consciousness and our word returns to us as faith, justifying our method.

Remember that there is no word that does not produce an effect of one sort or another, that some form of expression must of necessity take place for every word, and that if we persist in asking for anything, even our little faith will get results. There is an illuminating example of this in the man of whom Jesus spoke who secured the loaves of bread because of his "unblushing persistence." And Isaiah says, "Ye that make mention of the Lord, keep not silence, and give him no rest, till he establish" it. Every demand we make gets some answer. How much greater, then, shall be the scope of that answer when we persistently ask! Day by day, we erect the walls of our holy temple of peace; and each stone is the symbol of some word spoken often in the dark night of our soul and with but little faith. Yet that faith is the first glimmering of our dawn, and soon the rising sun shall flood our souls with the radiance of a day that never ends.

CHAPTER 2: THE LAW AND GOD

FAITH IN CONTROL OF NATURAL FORCES

THE law is not God. We often learn of those who are kept from the Truth and all the good it would otherwise bring into their lives through the fear that in some way they will lose the personal contact with God, and we would like to free those "who through this fear are all their lives kept in bondage."

While we claim to employ the law, we neither "manipulate it nor God." We simply learn how to apply the right factors to the law so that it can operate for us itself directly and without interference. Law is not synonymous with God. The word "God" is used to express the sum-total of all we mean by deity. It is a much-abused word and may mean much or little according to the concept. A highly-cultured Christian would have a very different concept of God from a Bedouin of the desert, or even an Arab of our own streets. Yet each might sum up all he means by deity in the one word God. (Or Allah.)

God is both the impersonal creative Mind, the Life, Love, and Wisdom in which we live, and also the Spirit or Intelligence conscious of being; — conscious of its power to act and consciously directing its own action. These are attributes of personality; and, as such a being, God may be spoken of as "He." This also explains the esoteric use of the masculine gender to denote the positive, creative, or life-giving function of spirit.*

Law is simply God's way of acting. Above the law is the Intelligence that acts through it. In fact, in the absolute sense there is no law. That means that Spirit simply acts as it chooses without reference to any idea of law, or any consciousness of it on Its own part. But, since Spirit is perfect harmony, every act fits every other act with perfect order; and man, viewing the expression of God's thought, calls it law. Viewed from the absolute, then, there is no law; viewed from the relative, or man's limited modes of vision, all is law. The seer has truly said, "All's

34

love, yet all's law"; and yet that is only from man's point of view. He cannot act independent of the law nor need he try because the law is beneficent and full of life.

Law, then, is, from man's point of view, simply the instrument through which God acts to perform his purpose. His acts are generic or along certain definite lines or tendencies. As law, these tendencies are impersonal and without individual purpose. No amount of personal or impassioned pleading on our part will persuade deity to act outside of its law, since it can "do above all we can ask or think" within the law. The law seems inexorable only as we strive to reverse its workings or plead for favors contrary to its nature.

ANSWER TO PRAYER

Does this, then, exclude Deity from answering our prayers? By no means, but the way it will answer them is already established. Do I mean, then, that God can and will set aside the order of nature to answer the prayer of faith? What do you mean by the "order of nature"? You say that it is natural law; for example, that man cannot walk on the water, he cannot rise into the atmosphere, he cannot break the law of the attraction of gravitation, he cannot still the storm nor cause the wind to cease.

(*See my "Being and Becoming," pages 22-23, and "The Law of Mind in Action," pages 166 to 171 and 179-185, for Personality of Spirit)

Yet Jesus walked on the water, rose in the air, and stilled the storm. Psychical research has proven beyond any doubt that there are powers in man which enable him to rise by some unseen power of levitation, to cause objects to move about in the air without physical support, and thus to act according to some fuller law of the attraction of gravitation. Does man, then, break these natural laws? NO; he simply acts in consonance with some deeper law with whose powers and nature he is as yet unfamiliar. Could he, then, still the storm?

"Why should it not be possible to cause the rain to fall or cease? A storm is due to certain conditions of barometric pressure, the rain is governed by certain fixed laws of pressure and heat; and these laws are governed by Mind. If, then, man could get into the right relation with this Mind, he could hope to govern the activity of the pressure and heat. He could not cause it to stop raining if the natural physical conditions were still in force; that is, he could not break the physical or lower law; but he could transcend it by getting in touch with the force that controls the natural physical conditions." Divine Mind would then act to stay the storm, not apart from its law but in accordance with it. And the further possibility should not be overlooked, that man himself can impress the idea of the change on the Cosmic Mind or Law which results in the change desired. Prayer would then be scientific because it would be in harmony with law throughout.

BIBLE SUPPORT OF FAITH IN CONTROL OF NATURAL FORCES

Such possibilities cannot be denied by those who accept the Bible with any degree of completeness whatever. Many cases are recorded of the control of natural forces, both in the Old Testament and the New, but always by men of great spiritual force like Elijah, who brought the rain after the drought, and Jesus who walked the waves. It is very evident, then, that the control of these things is not due to power to break the law but intelligent use of some law of mind or spirit above common knowledge. And it is equally plain that if one man can do these things, it is inherently possible for all men. Faith seems to be the essential element; but faith is merely a confident attitude of expectancy. Such a confident attitude is the idea, impression, or mental image which is given to the Cosmic Mind, which then acts upon it by the law of its nature.

Such extraordinary power as this could never be acquired save by men of the deepest spiritual character, — that is, those whose keenness of mental perception and idealism would prevent them from ever wanting to use their power for other purposes than the good of all. The history of the world is full of cases of answered prayer in the control of natural forces; but these answers came about through law, — the law that "according to your faith it is done unto you." In other words, there was sufficient expectation and desire for the common good, to move the Cosmic forces. Faith can move mountains, literally. That mountains are not moved is no proof to the contrary.

GOD GIVES WHAT WE ASK IN FAITH

Thus to have faith in the law is not to dishonor God by seeking to manipulate Him, but to honor Him by believing that He not only can but desires to rule His world in such a way as to give man the greatest freedom and joy. This He can best do by putting into the mind of man himself the power to initiate the train of causation which is to bring him the desired good. Faith is this power. Prayer is this power put into expression. Without it, man would be bound by natural forces; and his freedom would be only seeming. With it, he may rise to heights and destiny beyond even the imagination of the present hour. And any of us who view intelligently the discoveries of modern science and psychology, to say nothing of psychic research and the vision of the metaphysician, ought to be able to dream of that time to come, here on this very sphere, when man, having risen in mind and character to those levels of consciousness which make him worthy, shall be using forces so much finer than any known to the present hour that he shall literally live in a new heaven and a new earth while still in the body.

Meanwhile, do not leave to another day nor another person the glorious possibilities that lie inherently within you. Again with Jesus declare, "As the Father hath life in Himself, so hath He given it to the son to have life in himself. Whosoever believeth in me (takes my word to be true), from within him shall flow streams of living water." Declare for yourself this truth, — "I am endowed with all the nature and powers of the Son of God. I am a spiritual being possessed of unlimited resources. 'All that the Father hath is mine.' 'Whoso calleth on the name of the Lord shall be saved.' 'If he shall call upon me, I will answer him; I will be with him in trouble; with long life will I satisfy him and show him my salvation.' This I now affirm to be true of myself; and from this hour, in infinite faith in God, I shall go forward to do the work He has given me to do and to draw from heaven the high gifts that belong to me as His child."

CHAPTER 3: HOW TO DEMONSTRATE FAITH

FAITH is a confident attitude of mind; it is to feel assured that our "word will become flesh" ; that our thought will register in Creative Mind and take on a body; that when we say, "I am made whole," the Creative Energy will bring forth health. There are those who sit in the silence and declare the truth of life, who at some point in the treatment get a positive mental assurance that the work is, as they say, "done." They mean by that that they have reached the point in consciousness where they know that their thought has begun its work on the substance of mind to make the thing they want. Michael Angelo says, "Let me make an angel from this stone"; and he imagines how the angel will appear and begins to carve. He feels sure of the value of his vision, of his power to execute it, and that out of the unformed substance a struggling angel will emerge. So we take the unformed substance of Mind, dream the dream of our desired good, and believe that our thought will bring forth into form that for which we long. This belief is so certain in some minds that the healer will tell you when his work is done. Jesus knew that the work of raising Lazarus was accomplished in mind; even before he spoke the audible word, and declared, "I thank Thee, Father, that Thou nearest me always."

In Chapter I, we have shown how to go to work to demonstrate faith in just the way we would demonstrate health or success. But the subject is so important to us all that it will be of value here to show more of the process by studying how the mind works.

It is necessary to recall how retentive the mind is Just as nothing can be lost from the Infinite Consciousness, so nothing can ever be lost from your deeper reservoirs of mind. You never forget anything. The objective, or reasoning activities of mind, may lose touch with the things you want to remember; and you say, "I have forgotten." But have you? Let us suppose that it is a stanza of verse. You begin, "Break, break, break, on thy cold gray stones, O sea, And I would that my

38

tongue could utter . . ." and there you stop. What is that other line? You have a faint recollection of it. You can almost get it, but not quite. You run over the foregoing lines again and again but without result. You go to bed. The next morning you awake and the first thing you think of is the "forgotten" words,

"I would that my tongue could utter
The thoughts that arise in me."

Out of the subterranean depths of consciousness, long-neglected thoughts arise in you. By subtle trains of association, you bring them to the surface of the mind. Science says that no mental impression is ever lost.

THE FAITH YOU ALREADY HAVE

Let us suppose, therefore, that you have thought many thoughts that are full of faith. You have had faith in many things, just as you have now. You have had faith in the Bible as the wonderful Word of God. You have faith in the promises you have found there. You have faith in the love of the Father. You have faith in the love of your own family and friends. You have faith in your country. You have faith in a dollar-bill that you can get something in exchange for it. You have faith in your food, that it will strengthen your body. You have faith in the electric current, that it will take your car to the end of the line. You have faith in your own mind, that it can think rationally. You have faith in your ability to make things, or do things. Running over the list of your faiths, your confident attitude of expectancy about things of which you can have no immediate proof, how many you find! Faith is utter certainty about things of which you cannot in the nature of the case have any absolute proof. But you are sure of them. You live by faith. Without faith it would be impossible to exist for one moment in a world of things.

See, then, what faith you have already! Is it not wonderful? Do you not already have faith about nearly everything! Is not the aggregate of your faith greater than the aggregate of your doubt? Of course it is!

Nor is this all, for you are surrounded by thought-forces of faith. People with whom you are associated have faith. Some of them may have much more faith than you in some directions. Suppose, for example, that one has a great success consciousness, while yours is very low. That consciousness exists for you as a great example of the faith that you desire. More than that, that consciousness may become a distinct impression upon your own mentality, if you desire it. Again another has the consciousness of health, though not of prosperity. Viewing his health consciousness, you may claim that you share in it, and thus put yourself in the current of his thought.

The very universe is full of the thoughts and utterances of faith of the faith-full of all time. No word ever escapes from the eternal ethers or Divine Mind; and every thought that has gone forth to bless still lives in the frictionless medium of mind. Like birds, they flock to the window that is open to receive them.

We see, then, that everywhere there is encouragement for us: in the infinite resources of Mind; in the memories of all the faiths we have had; in the minds of others; in the very air. When the cry goes forth, "Increase my faith," it is the conviction or faith that there are others whose heightened faith can be ours, whose larger consciousness may be impressed upon our own. How, then, shall we go intelligently to work to secure all these benefits that await us on every hand?

DEMONSTRATING FAITH THROUGH
CLAIMING IT

To awaken our own consciousness to larger faith, we must, therefore, call upon all these resources. And this is as simple as any other demonstration. Simply declare, " I have perfect faith; and I am receptive to every thought of true faith anywhere."

The result of this statement will be to set up a magnet in the mind to attract all the helpful, hopeful, optimistic faith-thoughts within and without. You have declared that you have faith. The mind takes that as its picture-model. It begins to collect out of the hidden reservoirs of memory all the faiths of yesterday. It assembles them in orderly array, prepared to march against the army of your fears and erect the temple of your faith. Silently the thought, "I have faith in the power of my word; I have the healing consciousness, "begins to take upon it the body of which it is the soul. This word becomes the law of life for your mind, "I have faith; I am confident of the success which shall attend my every word." Even as you sleep, the sleepless mind goes on to build your temple, begins to "utter the thoughts that arise in you." As you scan the pages of books and magazines, there come forth to greet your eye the pictures of beautiful deeds and faith. You do not see the accounts of infidelity, shamefully featured as "news," but only the finer and more glorious acts of men. As you listen to the voices of the multitude, you do not hear jar nor jangle, fear, nor fault; you hear only those who speak words of comfort and who look with even eye of faith out onto life's landscapes. You become selective of the best because you have declared, "I have faith." Thus you draw to you thoughts that are inspiring and hopeful. You become a center for the attraction and radiation of faith. Through the open doors of mind and heart come the songs celestial, "Faith is the victory that overcomes the world." Thus faith can be demonstrated, thus you come at last to have the faith for which you long to make your home in the Heart of the Infinite. Daily declare, "I have this supreme wisdom, this mighty faith; I am at one with all faith; I am safe in the Infinite Mind of God." And, "according to your faith it shall be done unto you."

CHAPTER 4: THE NEW FAITH IN FAITH - HOW TO DEVELOP IT

THOUGHTS of themselves become things, and every mental attitude produces an effect of some kind. We are therefore constantly demonstrating the thing we do not want by thinking how much we do not want it. The bad that comes to us is simply the expression of wrong thinking. Malignant diseases are as much a matter of demonstration as their cure. A "cure" does not deal with the disease. It has nothing to do with the disease. The true healer never thinks, " I am healing disease. " He says, "I am knowing the truth." The disease, which is the expression of your faith in disease, vanishes before your faith in health.

Every disease ought to be a living proof of the creative principle. That inharmony thoughts can and do produce cancer ought to demonstrate the power of mind. You say, "I believe in the power of thought to produce physical results. I believe that thoughts make things. I even confess that my sickness is due to wrong thinking. And if I could make only one demonstration, I would have perfect faith hereafter."

Here you are illogical, for you admit that your disease is itself a demonstration. It is the result of your thought. So you have already demonstrated — what you do not want ! Now have faith in your power to make another — of the kind yon want!

Look about you and ask yourself this question, "Do I know of anything that exists independent of mental causation? Is not mind back of everything I see? Is not everything made by mind out of the substance of mind? Does not consciousness control creation, and is not the "thought father to the act"? Then consider what faith is. Faith is your own thought instinctively realized. Faith is the assurance in your own mind that your own thought will bring forth its own creation.

Since thought starts every creation and is backed up by all the mind and all the power there is, can your thought lack creative force? IT

CANNOT! Declare this truth: "I have faith in faith. I have faith in myself. I have faith in creative activity. I have faith in the outcome of my own faith. I am full of quiet confidence. I am calm. I am serene. I am confident. 'Thou wilt keep him in perfect peace whose mind is stayed on Thee.'"

CHAPTER 5: DEVELOPING FAITH THROUGH FEELING

FAITH is, in fact, a matter of feeling. Since we bring into expression just what we think, it is necessary to have as clear an image as possible; and this image is, of course, often blurred by the way we feel at the time of speaking the word. For this reason, we must work to eliminate the thought of pain or poverty from the mind and feeling. If pain rises up to protest against our statement and to deny its truth, we refuse its subtle suggestion. As a matter of fact, we are endowed by nature with the power of inhibiting pain. Pain is the incoming vibration over the sensory nerve to tell us that there is something wrong in the part of the body in question. These nerves are created by the ego-self to protect the body so that it may survive in an objective world. The pain is merely a warning of the intelligent cell-life that its existence is threatened. But having done that, the function of the pain is past; and the strong will can inhibit it for a while. You can refuse to accept the incoming sensation. All the sensation the body has, you give to it; you can also take it away. Ether, or mind, is a substance without qualities or feeling until consciousness gives feeling to it. Your body is made of the substance of mind and has pain only because of the self-conscious intelligence which lies within it and functions through it.

You do this, first, by withdrawing your consciousness from the part affected, through an act of will. Then you heal it through an act of faith. To withdraw consciousness is simply to say, " I will no longer accept this pain. "

Then, you can go on with your mental work of healing and get the unblurred vision. A good time to heal is in the morning, because you usually are free at that time from any sense of weariness or pain. A few minutes of undisturbed quiet in bed give one a sense of luxury and ease in body. Take that time to declare the truth. During the day, declare it often, not merely when the sickness reminds you of it but when you are feeling fairly well.

Do not allow yourself to fear that the pain will come back. "But," you say, "it has come back before; and I cannot help dreading it now." Can you not see that, if you have once overcome it so that you are free at this present moment, you can do the same again? Why borrow trouble? One woman said, "I am feeling well now; but I hate to feel well, because I always feel sick after I feel well." She set the law for herself; and she got what she felt she would.

Erase from your mind all doubt of the issue and take your stand on the truth, "I am a child of God. I have within me all the powers of my Father. I am free as He is free. I feel deeply the life of Spirit within me; and I shall fear no evil for Thou art with me."

DENIAL

A true denial is not the statement of a negative, for the statement of a negative is a positive. To state that there is a nothing, and then to make an attempt to heal it, is to make it a something. If there isn't any isn't, why treat that isn't? To deny disease is to say that there isn 't any disease to deny. To call it an illusion and then to give a treatment to get rid of the pain of the illusion is in itself an illusion. How do you know but that the treatment itself is an illusion?

To state that one lives in a world of illusions is mental assassination, for it plunges us at once into a dream-life and an unreal world wherein we lose all of our bearings. It is virtual insanity; and the crazy man playing at George Washington is as fortunate as we who only dream fantastically. To state that all is illusion is to state that there is nothing upon which to base reason at all. Then the reason by which you state the illusion is itself an illusion, and so is the statement. Thus confusion is doubly confused by a system of denials that affirms that there is a nothing which is so much of a something that we have to get rid of it.

And it is just as unreasonable to say that it is something if we like it, but nothing if we do not like it; that wealth is something; and poverty is nothing. And yet we are poor. Poverty is as much an experience as wealth. Everything is an experience; and therefore we have to find the solution of our problem, not in denying the experience but by changing it. Instead of allowing the unpleasant experience to occur, we must substitute a pleasant one. In the same way, dyspepsia is as much an experience as a well-digested potato. It is produced by the some process, — thought acting upon the intelligence of the stomach.

Spirit or mind is the substance which passes into the mould which we provide; and if we have a disagreeable experience, the way to get rid of it is to change the thought.

True denial, therefore, is simply to refuse to let the feeling of sickness or poverty take possession of us. We have to refuse to accept the impression. We inhibit or cut it off. We do not say, "I am not sick. I do not have disease. I do not have a material stomach, therefore I cannot have dyspepsia." We do say, — "I refuse to think anything but health. I will feel no pain. I will admit into mind only thoughts of life and health." We refuse to recognize the sensation of pain. Suppose there is such an experience as pain, "It shall not come nigh thee." Only with thine eyes shalt thou behold and see the reward (painful consequences) of the wicked (those who think in a warped and crooked manner).

To deny, therefore, merely refuse to admit destructive thoughts. Sternly put your mind under control and think constructively. I like the negro-woman who said to the dealer,

"Is you got any aigs?"

"I ain't said I ain't," he replied.

"I ain 't ast you, ' Is you ain't .' I ast you ' is you is.' Is you?"

If we are positively positive instead of positively negative, we can afford to forget the whole struggle of the mind that involves itself in denials and affirmations. Simply state positively what you want, utterly disregarding what you do not want; and it shall be done unto you even as you will. We get what we demand and what we expect.

CHAPTER 6: HOW TO HAVE FAITH IN YOUR HEALING WORD

WHEN we at last get a clear vision of truth, we begin to see and feel everything in a different way from, before. Truth is knowledge that we live in the invisible world of mind and that out of it everything that we can know in a material world is made in response to the Creative Word. It was of this truth that Jesus said, "Ye shall know it; and it shall make you free." The same spirit appears in all things. The same substance is in the flaming sunrise, the flying bird, and the flowering bush. The one substance composes your body, your environment, and your wealth. One Mind brings into expression the mole and the man, the mountain and the sea. Each thing that we see comes forth out of this one and the same Mind, and in each still lingers the intelligence of its source. Each thing has its soul. The soul is spirit individualizing itself to become the sustaining principle of that thing. And so long as spirit is conscious of itself as a rose, the rose endures. When the soul is withdrawn, the petals fall; yet, as the thought of God is infinite, who shall say whither the soul of the rose flies?

But man is more than the rose, for he is conscious of himself. He knows that he is spirit. He realizes himself as at one with the All-Intelligence. He is more than a thought. His body is the form thought has taken; but he, the self, is the thinker of the thought.

Conscious of himself as at one with the Creative Intelligence, he must then seek how he may reproduce Its activity in the control of his own conditions and affairs. He must awaken to his powers. He must learn to use the creative word. He must put forth his thought that it may embody itself in fitting form. He must know that he needs but "to speak the word only and my servant shall be healed" His word is the image or picture of his desire. The more faith he has in it, the better the results; but no word lacks power. Creative Mind begins to act on every word that is spoken.

CHOOSING WHAT YOU WILL HAVE

You do not have to make anything. Mind makes it. You have only to speak the word. What is it that you want? You must know that. What will you have? You are the chooser. Definitely decide on what you want. Then as definitely declare that it is "done unto you now." Do not think of yourself as struggling to make something. Just think of yourself as the one who is starting the train of causation that is to bring you something. Put your word out with confidence, knowing that it is not you but Spirit that is to do the work. "Ye shall know the truth; and the TRUTH SHALL MAKE YOU FREE." The law of mind does all the work.

Today declare, "I have faith in the power of the law. I believe that all is mind, everywhere manifesting itself as the life and soul of things. I believe that all things and forms are responsive to my will because of the intelligence of the One Mind that dwells in them. I believe that my word goes forth to control my conditions. I believe that my word is the soul of the thing I desire and takes on its body when and where it is best. I believe that my word has power. I believe that my word registers in Creative Mind. I know now that this word that I am speaking is being taken up by the All-Mind to be acted upon with all power and all intelligence. I have faith in the power of my word to find its place in the Creative thought. I have faith that it is there. The work is already done in my own consciousness. I feel satisfied. It is done."

Then rest your case with the Creative Mind. "The truth shall make you free."

CHAPTER 7: FAITH IN THE GREAT WITHIN

ONE DAY AT A TIME

LEARN to live life day by day. Never live tomorrow except by happy anticipation. To dread tomorrow is to demonstrate a tomorrow to be dreaded. If today is not all you wish it to be, rise above it in thought and declare your faith in all the good to come. Then it must come. To bewail the present hour is to sow the seed of new distresses. Laugh if you can, sing if you can. And if you cannot sing, then shout. My brother used to say when he heard me about the house, "It seems to me that I have heard the same words to a different tune." Never mind, the tune is in the heart. What is your heart-song? Let it ring out today. Cheer up, the best is yet to be.

Every day there are men who die because they think they are going to be hurt. Fright takes their breath away. There are still others who are wearing themselves out trying to make the world all right. The world is already all right, and your fear about it will only be a contribution toward making it wrong. The way to make the world right is to be right yourself. Then you will at least "brighten the corner where you are." If everybody does that, he is doing his part. It is a good deal better to be the message than it is to tell it.

Instead of trying to set the world right, set the ideals of your own life right. Work out every problem from within. All growth is from within. The way to change things is to change in consciousness first of all. May heaven pity the rest of the world if we, who know the truth, are living anything else than the ideal today. If we, who know the truth of life, find it necessary to turn to outside agencies to make things right, what shall the struggling multitudes do! Dare to fling yourself on the bosom of the Law. Dare to say, "It shall be done unto me." Dare to believe that you can better get results through faith than through struggle. Stop struggling! Struggle raises resistance, and resistance brings upon you the very evil you deplore.

I do now declare my faith in today. I know that there is nothing wrong in the eternal order; and the changing world is the changing thought of man. I will therefore align myself with the eternal order.

CHAPTER 8: HOW TO DEVELOP FAITH IN YOURSELF

SELF-CONFIDENCE

IS there any place, time, or event in which the One Mind is not operative? Are you not in that mind? Is there in the One Mind any point where there is less than the All-Intelligence and the All-Power? Is not the One Mind evenly distributed through all space, time, things and men?

Of whom, then, are you to be afraid? Fear of others is a disrespect to the self. A proper estimate of the self is not only essential to true manhood and womanhood but also to comfortable living. Let us take time, if necessary, to dwell on the fact, "I am no less than the greatest or the wisest. That in him which makes him wise or great is also in me. His very greatness rests on my ability to recognize and appreciate his virtues. I could not do this unless there were inherent in me the same greatness. That I can appreciate his qualities is a tribute to my own."

Am I less than this man because today he has money and I am poor? He is no richer than I in possible resources; but he has mined more of his wealth. He is no nobler born than I; he has manifested more of his nobility. His position and honor are the output of his faith in himself. They have come to him because he demanded them. They are the response to his thought and ambition. They are the tribute to himself. But they are things which I also can express for myself.

When we approach a man with dread, do we, after all, fear the man himself? No, we fear things, names, position, wealth, varnish, velours and vases, — the glamor by which he is surrounded. Knowing these to be the expression of his own rich consciousness, why let them stand between you and him as obstacles? "When you make your next approach, GO TO SEE THE MAN HIMSELF. A true estimate of the SELF places you on a level with all men.

"For there is neither East nor West,

Border, nor breed, nor birth;
When two strong men stand face to face,
Though they come from the ends of the earth."

You are just as strong, just as great, just as noble as you think you are when you become aware of the true self.

Thus we see that faith in ourselves comes from learning to estimate men and things in terms of spirit. Am not I on a level with Life Itself? Do I seek favors for which I cannot give value for value? Is not as much good to come to this man for his favors as to me who seek them? If I am full of fear, is it not virtually because I either lack confidence in my "goods" or myself? Fear of others is no less than fear of oneself. Then let me no longer go apologetically about. While truly honoring all men, I shall say, — "I, too, am a great soul. I, too, am a creative spirit. I, too, am noble. I, too, am success, and name, and fame. I am all men's comrade, worthy of all respect, expectant of fair treatment. I have faith in myself. " Fit yourself mentally by claiming your true nature. Put yourself in harmony with the man whom you wish to approach. On the level of spirit make your unity with him. Then go confidently forward. You cannot fail. Be true first of all to the nobility of your soul. Nobility bows to nobility; and the greatest will bow before the inherent splendor of the soul that is true to itself.

CHAPTER 9: HOW TO DEVELOP FAITH IN HAPPINESS

CHEER up. "These are the very words used by the Master Healer before He spoke the word of healing. You cannot be well while you are "in the dumps." Tears make fears; and fears make images; and images impress themselves upon the Law. The magic Mirror of Life catches the doleful face and gets this idea, "Everything is wrong, only the worst is expected." Then, since it puts forth into form just what is given to it in idea, we soon find our worst moods and fears realized. In the midst of darkness, you cannot afford to indulge your sorrow or your pessimism. Rouse yourself vigorously and thrust aside the ghostly specter of sadness. Put it off your pathway with a master's hand. Knowing the truth, you dare not do otherwise. You will master your emotions; you will control your thoughts.

To be downhearted is to be cowardly, it is to accept the buffets of life as the blows of fate. The bold-hearted receive the blow as a warning to themselves that they are off the highway and must get on again. To such, "every knock is a boost," for it urges them forward and demands more rigorous control of thought. We must learn to meet life with a smile and, bravely facing the storm, to declare our faith in the calm that follows. Never a storm has raged but has had its end! Never a loss or sorrow but peace came afterwards! Face into the storm and see the sun behind the cloud! Remember,

"Why wind-swept mountain-oaks endure,
When oaks in the vale are riven."

To weakly yield to the moods of depression, to bow humbly before the storm, is suicidal to the great soul. This is the moment to declare your divine rights. At this hour, let your soul arise in majesty. It is not fate but yourself that you are facing now. Fight it out to a decisive issue.

"The fault, dear Brutus, lies not in our stars,
but in ourselves,

That we are underlings."

Claim happiness out of the Universal. It is there in abundance; but you must draw upon it. Spirit is ready to give; but we must take; nay, more, we must boldly demand. But of whom shall we demand? First, we must insist more with ourselves, "I shall have happiness and freedom. I will not despair. I will stop fearing. I am not afraid. I do believe. I will not accept anything but the best. I am master of my own emotions." Second, we must call forth the full measure of joy from the Universal by expecting it. We must expect more. "I do now turn to the exhaustless supply for wisdom and happiness. Joy belongs to me; and I claim it. God is joy. Life is joy. Let every inharmony now pass away from me. I expect the best to come to me, and come now. Only the best can come, only the best is here."

In sorrow and loneliness, in sickness and want, the great need of the soul is that calm poise that refuses to accept conditions as they are. Refuse to despair! Turn to the Infinite and thus declare: "My faith is made perfect in Thee. As Thy child, I am heir to the best. I abide in Thy love. Thou hast made no place for sorrow to the soul that flings itself out upon faith. Though today I am in the midst of darkness, yet am I in the light. Today, I summon forth from heaven the best and the highest. I take joy as my right. Let love and peace descend upon my soul. Let me rise in exultation of spirit. I am heir of all the ages. I am joy itself. "'I am the resurrection and the life. He that believeth on me, from within him shall flow streams of living water.'"

CHAPTER 10: KEEPING YOUR FAITH IN THE WORLD

WE lose faith in the world only because we see its weaker side. We could never lose faith if we saw only the strength and goodness everywhere. There is good all about us, if we will look for it. Some one said once to a certain woman, "I believe you would see something good in the Devil." To which she replied, "We might all admire his persistency." We find in life just what we are looking for. A teacher once told her pupils to bring pictures to her of scenes in which there was light. One of the little boys from the slum-district brought a postal card; and the teacher, looking at it in anger, called the boy to her and said, "How dare you bring a filthy picture like this?" Tears came to his eyes; and he said, "Don't you see, teacher? There's the moon? There's the moon!" And, shining through the dirty pane of glass, the teacher saw the crescent moon. The eyes of the boy had seen only light there.

The way to keep your faith in the world is to look at the good the world is doing. Men are getting better all the time. Character is far in advance of any previous day. The saintly fathers of the church of a former generation did not think it cruel to inflict tortures upon human beings at which the meanest criminal of our day would shudder. The conscience and character of men is steadily growing better. If you don't think so, it is because you are looking too long at what you should not see. If you have a tendency toward scepticism of the good, buy the three little monkeys. Make them your motto, "I will see no evil; I will speak no evil; I will hear no evil." After a while, you will have faith in the world. "Why do newspapers make their principle stock-in-trade the sensational murder or divorce?" you ask. Why, how do you know they do? How do I know they do? We have seen it. We are like the boy at prayers. "Teacher," he said, "Joseph kept his eyes open while you prayed." Everybody is doing it more or less — seeing the evil, feeding on it, and therefore demanding it. The newspapers will stop publishing that sort of thing when we get to the point where we won't read it.

Then, when we stop seeing evil, we shall stop experiencing it. Why is there often a "crime wave" in large cities? It is the contagion of example. One sees and hears what another is doing; and he goes and does likewise. Recently a boy hanged himself over a bathtub and died, imitating a hero at the "movies."

To keep your faith in the world, look for good. You cannot look two ways at once; and "if your eye be single, your whole body will be full of light." The world grows better as we grow better. We see only those things that most interest us. We must therefore seek higher and finer interests if we are to have faith in the world. Never forget that the world becomes to you just what you become to it. The law of mind is that we get out of the Universal just what we put into it. If, therefore, you would have faith in the world, turn your mind to the good there is in it. Soon you will begin to attract around you those who are most like you in mental attitudes. They, too, will see the good; and, as you will be mutually associated, you will soon find that you have faith in the world because you not only saw the good and thought the good but you have now actually demonstrated the good.

Declare your faith; and it shall be justified by the fact. "I am surrounded only by the finest and best people. They are people whom I can trust. " No one is going to go back on their word with you; no one is going to deceive you; no one is seeking your injury. You are protected by the inviolability of your own soul. Only these things can reach you to which you are mentally open. So, "Today I am filled with perfect peace and faith in everybody and everything. Life is worth while for it is under my control; and I can be what I will to be."

CHAPTER 11: PRAY AS YOU RUN

THERE is no "place" in consciousness. There are only states of mind. You are no nearer the source of life and supply in the closet or before the altar than you are on the highway or in the market place. There is only one "point of contact;" and that is within your own soul. It is true that every place has its atmosphere and that the constant presence of spiritual thinkers and thinking will produce a certain uplifting aura so that we are at once led to worship by the mental suggestion about us: yet, at the same time, we are not to suppose that we need be dependent upon it. The greatest seers have usually been those who went out into the desert and made their own atmosphere and then came back and tried to keep it in the crowd; we must remember that each man carries his own atmosphere with him. You can carry "the secret place of the Most High" with you wherever you go, a pillar of cloud by day and a fire by night. Do not think that you must rush away to the closet or even stop going on.

Two little girls were on their way to school. They heard the bell. "Oh, we are going to be late," said one. "Let's kneel right down and ask God to save us from being late." "No, no," said the other. "Let's scud right along and pray as we run."

Spirit does much for you. It also does much through you. Be as ready for one as for the other. While you do not choose the way in which things shall come to you, you must not be asleep when Spirit calls on you to act for It in accomplishing your desire. Be Its instrument willingly. Laziness is as wrong on the one hand as struggle on the other. The drowning man who prays, "Lord, help me!" and doesn't try to swim, usually drowns. The Lord probably wants to act through that man's arms and legs. Put yourself in the attitude of receptivity to the divine guidance. Expect help. Find the way; and then go on!

It is not the prayer in the closet but action upon faith that gets results. Have faith and then act upon it. Do not deny by act and word in daily contact with life, all that you sought in the silence. One woman prayed, "Lord, remove that mountain. I know you can; and I want it out of the way." The next morning she got up and said, "There's that old mountain in the same place. I knew it wouldn't go." So we face the mountains of difficulty and say, "Let them pass away;" and then we go out to contradict in act and mind every thought of faith we have uttered. It is not an eloquent prayer but an eloquent faith that counts. The thoughts of all day are the ones that count. You cannot get results by "going over your denials and affirmations" and then continually talking and acting the opposite. It is the totality of your mental attitudes that give the results you get.

One of the best healers I know does much of her healing work right along with the usual activities of her daily life, when she "does" her dishes or makes the beds and sweeps, maintaining the truth all the time.

Work should be balanced by rest. We so easily swing to extremes! We owe it to ourselves to take times for rest and recreation. If your consciousness is low and you cannot "get hold of your case," while still going on with your daily work, then by all means stop working for a while. The mind continually full of cares and the attentions to business may refuse to react to higher thinking. Then shake off the dust of things and rest. There is always a way. If no way appears now, then demand it from the law. Make your first demand for leisure. Demonstrate leisure and then go on for health.

SLEEP AND HEALTH

Sleep will often help you in the work of regaining control of your body. During sleep, the body is taking on energy in just the same way that the electric car gets its batteries renewed during the night. The soul-self never sleeps and during the night it is drawing in reserve energies for the body. As you go to sleep at night, you may direct these energies to act in any portion of the body that you desire. Or you may direct that the soul-self shall bring more faith into your waking consciousness. While you are resting, continue to assert that the healing power is now restoring you. During rest and sleep, new energies are taking their place in the body: if, then, you consciously direct them, they will go to work to do what you require. You direct them simply by telling the soul-self what it is that you want it to do.

There is no better time to start the growth of the faith consciousness than when you are quietly resting or just before you fall to sleep. State firmly that you do have faith, that your faith is growing, that you will awaken with renewed hope and peace, and the sleepless self will carry your thought to the ultimate conclusion. You will then awake to new courage and a more positive attitude of expectancy. As soon as you awake, think how beautiful everything is, how well you are and will continue to be. In the morning you can give yourself perhaps the best treatment because you usually feel so refreshed that you do not have anything in consciousness to contradict your word.

"Still, still with Thee when early morning breaketh.
When the bird waketh and earth's shadows flee.
Fairer than the morning, lovelier than the daylight,
Shall rise the glorious thought, I am with Thee."

Fall asleep in the arms of the Infinite Love. Awaken to the song of the soul, "I am still with Thee." "I and the Father are one." "All power is given unto me in heaven and on earth."

CHAPTER 12: WEARING OTHER PEOPLE'S CLOTHES

YOU have now joined the ANCIENT AND HONORABLE ORDER OF DIVINE INDEPENDENCE.

You have associated yourself with the emancipated souls of all the ages. You have come under the direct mastership, the "Worthy Master" of your own soul. You acknowledge but one Supreme Ruler, God acting through your own soul and your own individuality. You are not aggressively independent. You do not flaunt your freedom in the faces of those who yet are bound. You do not exercise liberties that are mere license. You do not take occasion to criticise another man's living or ways of thought. You do not sneer at his religion nor his limitations in knowledge. You do not try to control anybody. You do not try to change anybody. Nobody is eternally lost for there is no place to lose them. There is but one Infinite Mind; and no one can fall out of it.

To be sure there are many who have lost their sense of direction; and you can help them. You can point out the path; but you must not try to walk it for anybody. That is to put them into bondage. What we do, who seek to lift up the "weak and faint-hearted," is to declare unto them a better way. We can help them to short-cut their experiences, to learn the truth without the bitter pain. Then, if they will hear and heed, they may avoid the pitfalls of life. If not, then they will have the experience that follows upon every wrong thought as well as every right one. Every thought is followed by some form of expression. If we like the expression, we call it good. If we do not like it, we call it bad. Then when the "bad" comes, we perceive it as the inevitable consequence of our thought and act. It is not a judgment, but a consequence, an experience. The experience sets us again on the Big Road.

If you and I can put others on the Big Road, then we can save them to that extent and no more. God cannot save a man more than that. That is enough. You are therefore safe in pointing out the best road;

but you are not to worry about him nor to try to force him to act the way you think is best. Wear your own clothes; and let him do the same.

No suit will fit two people with equal grace. You would not like to wear another man's coat nor another woman's dress. It will either be too loose or too tight. Having joined the Order of Divine Independence, let the other fellow belong to the society of his own choice. The greatest missionary this world will ever produce is the man who lives the life of the Exalted Ruler of his own soul. Men, seeing him, will enquire the secret of his life. Looking into his face, they will say, "Oh, that I may be like him!" Reveal the secret. The great man is he who lives the great life. In you is that potential great man. Your soul is as great as the greatest when it stands revealed in all its pristine glory. Let the God within come forth to greet his world. What wonders will burst upon the world when we all shall say, "Reveal thyself to me, Living One, not in the terms of my limited personality, but in the radiance of the God-self which now slumbers within." Then, shall the within be realized as greater than that without. " He that hath ears to hear, let him hear."

CHAPTER 13: I AM THAT BIG DEED NOW

KEEP your eye on what you want, not on what you don't want. I saw a little boy the other day riding a tricycle. He was pedaling along on the sidewalk. Off to his right, and well out of the way, was a telephone pole. He kept his fearful eye on the pole; and, when he came opposite it, he put his hand out to save himself. That act pushed him off the wheel. How often are your fears pushing you off the road! Keep your eye on the thing you want. It will help you to concentrate your mind, if you will write out a statement of the thing that you most want and demand and post it where you will see it oftenest. Try putting it on the mirror! Every time you see it, say, "That is what I am. That is what I have."

What shall the statement be? I do not know. What do you desire? Do you know? Then say it. "I am perfect health. I am spirit; and I am life. I am the resurrection and the life. I am above envy. I am generosity itself. Let the new and the better appear in my life. I am that big deed now. Spirit guides me with Its perfect wisdom."

GO AFTER SOMETHING BIG

We all ought to rise out of the smallness of things. There is no one who cannot do some one big thing. Think about it often. What shall you contribute to the world? What shall you do that is distinctive?

You are different from any other man or woman in the world. Show your own divine individuality. Declare daily, "The way is open to me. I see with enlarged vision. I am that big self now. My mind is open to the big thing. I will do it. I am at one with the biggest and the best."

Some morning you will awaken to find yourself a contributor to the world's thought. Out of the limitless possibilities, the untapped resources of Mind, you shall bring forth your individual gem of truth. You are that great one now. You are the blessing and the blessed among men, for you are great with a true greatness. Through you has been born into the world's thought some finer thought or deed. Thus you have played your part in drawing forth from the Matchless Mind of the Infinite, the inspiration by which man shall rise to heights divine. Thus you are a co-worker with Him.

CHAPTER 14: FAITH IN YOUR UNITY WITH GOD

FORGIVE YOURSELF

THE unpardonable sin is blasphemy against the Holy Spirit which "shall not be forgiven either in this world or in the world to come." "Why? Because, in the nature of the case, it cannot be. So long as you deny the reality, power, and presence of Spirit, or refuse to come into harmony with It, you automatically cut yourself off from Its benefits. To blaspheme is to declare against it. If you separate the belt from the driving-gear, the machinery will stop running. If you separate yourself in consciousness from Spirit and Life, you lose its driving power. Sin and evil are separation in consciousness from Truth and Life. Sickness and poverty are the impoverished state in which the Prodigal finds himself who tries to live apart from the Source of life and supply — the Father's house.

Health, wealth and love depend upon our faith in the Spirit and our allegiance to the law. Therefore, if you feel separated from good; if you are inclined to condemn yourself for past acts, saying, "This is just what I ought to expect," and accepting it as inevitable; if you submit meekly to suffering; if you think that your word lacks power because you have done what is wrong; if in any way you have a sense of separation from Spirit, then forgive yourself.

"The son of man hath power on earth to forgive sins." You are that son of man. You are daily forgiving the sins of others, why not your own? "I say ye are gods; and every one of you sons of the Most High." Heaven has already forgiven you, for Spirit cannot have a sense of separation from you since Spirit is all and can not be conscious of parts. In calm composure of soul declare, "I am in the Father and the Father in me; and I am perfected into one with all men, with Life Itself. I have a sense of perfect union. I do now make restitution to all men; I forgive all; I am forgiven. I am now received fully into the Father's Life. 'I and

63

the Father are one!'"

CHAPTER 15: FAITH IN THE CONTINUITY OF LIFE

THIS is the message of hope. Let faith abide in every heart. God is all. There is no place where He is not. There is no place outside of Him. There is no place away from him. Life is consciousness; and individual consciousness is our share in the Cosmic. We are waves running on the bosom of the infinite ocean. No crest shall toss so high but that, beneath, it rests upon the waters of Life itself. The "lost soul" is only the soul that has lost consciousness of its bearings and its relationship. It is not lost to the consciousness of God. No soul can ever lose consciousness of itself. To do so would be to annihilate God Himself, for it would rend Him into parts or leave a vacuum in Mind: both of which are inconceivable. God is all and cannot lose his identity. You are one with the Father.

Life, then, cannot be extinguished. The form may change but not the former. The spirit goes back to its home somewhere in the Infinite sea, but ever possesses the power to emerge again in form in the place and way its will and unfoldment shall decree. For a time, the loved one may be away from you, but how? Perhaps only in visibility. Perhaps there may come the day when all men shall behold their loved ones in the glory of the spiritual body even while we are still in the flesh. Certainly it is true that the thought of our dear ones can reach us and our thought reach them. And as the soul goes wherever the thought takes it, once we are freed from the body we shall join those whom we love by the mutual drawing of desire, just as our loved ones have already joined each other in that heaven land.

But, whether we receive word from beyond the grave or not, we must know that we are still in the thought of our beloved, even as they are in our thought. Their love can reach us. Ours can reach them. Cannot we trust them to the Infinite Love? The same sun shines on east and west alike. It shines on Jupiter, Saturn and the earth. The soul that has swung far into the orbit of Life is still as close to the Father as we; and the Same Father holds both it and us in the Infinite Care.

Though I speed to some far goal
Unrevealed in spaces dim,
God is everywhere, my soul;
Thou mayst fly, yet rest in Him!!

CHAPTER 16: FAITH IN GOD

NOW can God allow it? Can there be a God at all and permit such things to happen?" That is the age-long cry of despair. It is the natural appeal of the soul that has been taught that God is judge and executioner. There could be no more awful conception of the Father! The Christ-message reveals Him differently. He is the Good Shepherd leading His sheep out of the darkness of the mountains; the Comforter who will never leave us: the Peace-Bringer, the Father, the Lover.

It is not God, but ourselves who bring the judgment and the execution upon us:

For judgment is the pain we bear while yet we sin,

The retribution of the soul at war with self and God

While yet the war goes on! But, leaving sin, we leave the judge behind

And pass from death to life; from hate to love; from pain to joy;

Because the good is there!

The law is that as we sow, we reap. If we "sow to the wind, we reap the whirlwind." Judgement and punishment are the inevitable consequence of wrong-doing. The judge is the law. We make our own hell. How often, since I awoke to the greater truth of life, have I been thankful for this: "I made my own hell.

It was not made for me. Since I made it, I can get out of it. If it had been made for me, I could not get out. I not only can get out of hell; but, by the same process, I can get into heaven. The kingdom of heaven is within me."

KARMA

Nor need I fear some awful karmic law. It is true that wrong thinking and acting bring suffering; but, if I place myself in harmony with Spirit which is Wisdom, I can intuitively avoid wrong thinking. If my karma is made by thought, it can be overcome by changing the thought.

I will therefore change my thinking. No longer will I submit to the fatalism of supposing that I am bound forever in the toils of my past mistakes. By the laws of my own being, I am kept from the error of wrong thinking; and today I escape the pains of the past by recognizing that they are merely the arrows that point me to the true path, and by changing my thought. The true law of Karma merely warns us that we reap as we sow and is our friend, for it directs our thought to constructive issues. The false law of Karma is a fatalistic acceptance of suffering and of the inevitable. Such a law can be swallowed up by the higher law of true thinking.

I demand freedom, joy, and peace. I accept only the best. I expect only the best. I am free with a glad freedom. Let my voice ring out with the gladness of life, for I am forever kept on the pathway of the soul. "Thou wilt keep him in perfect peace whose mind is stayed on thee."

HAVE FAITH IN GOD

Today I will turn in faith to God. He did not make my suffering. He made me a free agent. He said, "Choose what you will." Thus he gave me individuality; and, if I choose wrongly, it is not His fault. So I turn to Him in confidence. He loves me. He will guide me. I, therefore, put myself into an attitude of loving union with Him. I open my eyes to see the good; I open my ears to hear the good; I open my heart to accept the truth. God is Wisdom, Love, and Truth. I am now receptive to guidance from on high.* I turn my thoughts in love and faith to the All-Good, and know that "when He, the Comforter is come, He shall teach me all things and guide me in the way of truth." I shall therefore be free of error in thought and act. So do I fling myself on the bosom of the Infinite, for

"Behind the dim unknown,
Standeth God within the shadows, keeping watch above his own."

(Note. See pages 172-178, "Law of Mind in Action," by the author, for instruction on intuitive guidance.)

CHAPTER 17: WHAT DO YOU EXPECT?

THERE is war for the warlike. There is peace for the peaceful. There is hope for the hopeful. There is faith for the faithful. There is plenty for the plentiful. There is happiness for the joyful. There is a song for the singer; there is love for the lover; there is God for the worshipper. There is a sun for children of the day and a cloud for children of the night. For him who would be rich, there is riches; and he who expects nothing shall equally be blessed by the law, for verily his faith shall have its reward. "He sends his sun and his rain upon the just and the unjust, the evil and the good."

Each of us makes his own sunrise and his own sunset. Each soars or crawls as his thought decrees. He takes the wings of the morning and mounts to Pleiades, or the feet of the mole and burrows in the earth. He walks uprightly fearing no man or meekly bends before every pretender to his throne. He goes forth with fear and meets his fate, or with courage and is hailed as conqueror. He laughs and the world laughs with him; he weeps and all the world's in tears.

Life is a comedy to the optimist and a tragedy to the pessimist. No loving heart but finds its mate. No hostile heart but finds its enemy. No fear but finds its devil; no faith but finds its God.

It is of the very nature of life and mind that every thought is matched by reality in two directions: it exists as an eternal possibility in the universal, or else we could not think it: it must come forth into form, for every thought expresses in its individual way. Clearness of thought, which is the image and persistency of the thought, which is faith, alone decree when and how completely it shall come. Every thought becomes a thing, but whether it is vital or still-born is governed by your faith.

This is the great inspiration of the new-old message of the Christ-conscious: you cannot conceive a desire but that it is matched by reality. The inventor who fashions an instrument never before seen, the sculptor who chisels a form never before conceived, are merely bringing into expression ideas that lie latent in the Mind of the Infinite. You cannot want anything but God wants it for you: you cannot expect anything but that that thing can and will come to you, IF YOU EXPECT IT ENOUGH.

What do you want! What do you expect? These are the decisive factors in the living of your life. Behind you lie the broken things of yesterday. Forget them. Before you is dawn and the day. What shall come forth out of the unrolled parchment of the future? It is for you to decide. You hold tomorrow in the hollow of your hand. God is on your side. Life is on your side. Eternity is on your side; Life never ends. All things are possible to him that believes. "Only have faith; and thy faith shall save thee." Believe, believe! EXPECT, EXPECT!!

FINIS

ABOUT THE AUTHOR

Fenwicke Lindsay Holmes (1883-1973) was a philosopher, speaker, lecturer, Congregational minister, and influential Religious Science leader. Holmes was born on a farm near Lincoln, Maine in 1883. He was married to Katharine Eggleston. During his life, he wrote more than twenty books. His teachings has influenced many people all around the world.

You might also like:

YOUR FAITH IS
YOUR FORTUNE

NEVILLE
GODDARD

Your Faith is Your Fortune
ISBN: 1479306150
ISBN-13: 978-1479306152

FEELING IS
THE SECRET

NEVILLE
GODDARD

Feeling is the Secret
ISBN: 1479309656
ISBN-13: 978-1479309658

HOW THE MIND WORKS

CHRISTIAN D. LARSON

How the Mind Works
ISBN-13: 978-1479385997
ISBN-10: 1479385999

HOW TO GET WHAT YOU WANT

ORISON SWETT MARDEN

How to Get What you Want
ISBN-13: 978-1480069985
ISBN-10: 1480069981

THE GAME OF LIFE
AND HOW TO PLAY IT

FLORENCE
SCOVEL SHINN

The Game of Life and How to Play It
ISBN-13: 978-1479355709
ISBN-10: 1479355704

BOTH RICHES
AND HONOR

PROSPERITY THROUGH
SPIRITUALITY

ANNIE RIX
MILITZ

Both Riches and Honor
ISBN-13: 978-1480060623
ISBN-10: 1480060623

Made in United States
Orlando, FL
24 November 2024

54370907R00046